THE WORK OF THE HOLY SPIRIT

Author of

Christian Doctrine
Revelation and God
The Gospel of Redemption
The Faith of the New Testament

THE WORK OF THE HOLY SPIRIT

A Treatment of the
Biblical Doctrine of the Divine Spirit

Walter Thomas Conner

BROADMAN PRESS

NASHVILLE, TENNESSEE

4216–18

Printed in the United States of America

*This book is dedicated
to the memory of H. E. Dana,
former student, colleague in teaching,
and friend to the end*

CONTENTS

PREFACE

For several years I have studied the subject and taught a course in the biblical doctrine of the divine Spirit. This book is the outcome of that study. No reader of the book will be more conscious than I am of the imperfection of the treatment. I should like to spend more time investigating and reflecting on the subject before sending the discussion out for others to read. But in a subject like this, if one waited until he was conscious that he had reached finality on all points, when would he speak? While I am conscious that I cannot speak with finality on all points, I do feel that I can speak with a measure of assurance on the main features of the biblical doctrine of the Spirit.

There is no area of Christian doctrine where thought and life need to be kept in close relation more so than in this doctrine of the Spirit. An abstract, speculative doctrine of the Spirit would not be worth much. Present-day American Christianity needs a deepening insight into spiritual realities. But along with this deepening insight must go an increased measure of Spirit-guided activity. Here thought and activity must mutually condition each other. Faith-informed and faith-guided activity will lead to deeper insight. Insight and activity must travel *pari passu*.

The list of books at the end is by no means exhaustive, as any student in the field will recognize. They are some from which I have obtained some help. Perhaps they will be of some aid to other students in the field.

My aim in this discussion is not to satisfy the scholar who wants an exhaustive treatment, but to stimulate and aid ministerial students, pastors, and others who need a measure of guidance in this field. So far as help from books is concerned, I think I have found as much, and in some respects more, help from discussions not directly treating this subject. Often indirect lighting is best. Sometimes direct lighting produces too much glare. Direct discussions of a subject are sometimes too narrowly based. In a general discussion of philosophy or theology one will sometimes get a better perspective of a particular subject like this than he will in a direct treatment of the subject.

I have dwelt all the way through on the practical bearing of the work of the Spirit on the life of man. I have not been concerned so much with the theoretical aspect of the matter as with the practical, hence I am calling the book, *The Work of the Holy Spirit.*

I am indebted to a number of friends for help in preparing this work. First of all, I acknowledge my indebtedness to President E. D. Head, of the Southwestern Baptist Theological Seminary, for practical encouragement and aid in several ways—especially with reference to the matter of time to do the work. Then I have received help from several members of the faculty, particularly Dr. Ray Summers of the Department of New Testament Interpretation, Dr. R. T. Daniel of the Department of Old Testament Theology, and Dr. Stewart A. Newman of the Department of the Philosophy of Religion. I am also obligated to two ladies for encouragement and help. My wife has been a constant help with sympathetic suggestions and constructive criticisms. The reader will be indebted to her for a style with a few less jolts to his literary sensibility than otherwise he would have suffered. She has been my most constant and helpful critic in preparing and revising the body of the discussion. Then I am conscious of a heavy debt of obligation to Miss Alta Lee Grimes, by whose patient and persevering efforts the manuscript has been typed and prepared for the printer. But she has been more than a typist. She has also made many helpful suggestions about the form and substance of the discussion.

I am indebted to my colleague in the Department of Theology, Dr. Charles A. Trentham, for the preparation of the indices.

W. T. CONNER

Fort Worth, Texas

CHAPTER 1

INTRODUCTION

In this book we are to consider the biblical character of the Holy Spirit. We will give some attention to the views of the Spirit as developed in church history, but we will seek to keep our discussion biblically centered all the way. The idea of spirit, or spirits, is not confined to biblical religion. There were and are spirits in abundance in other religions, but for the religious movement that grew out of the life, teaching, and redemptive work of Jesus Christ in the world, the idea of spirit is essential. But not just any conception of spirit will answer; it must be the conception of the Spirit of God as set forth in the Bible. For the justification of this position, that the biblical conception of the divine Spirit is essential to Christianity, we will have to rely upon our whole discussion that follows.

I

If our thought is to follow the lines laid down in the Bible, we will need to put stress on the doctrine of the Spirit. This is one of the most prominent ideas found in the Bible. In the second verse of the Bible, we find the author saying that the Spirit of God brooded on the face of the waters to bring order out of chaos. In the last chapter of Revelation (22:17), we find, "And the Spirit and the bride say, Come." All through the Bible this is a prominent idea. It is not as prominent in the Old Testament as in the New. As a matter of fact, there are large

[1]

stretches in the Old Testament where we find neither the term nor the experience and idea for which the term stands. Nevertheless, if we take the Bible as a whole, the idea of the divine Spirit is quite prominent. The doctrine of the Spirit stands for an indispensable phase of the Christian religion.

An idea in Christianity is not to be evaluated simply by the number of times that it is used in the Bible. We must take into account the experience for which it stands. Without question, the biblical doctrine of the Spirit of God stands for an indispensable element in our religion. In general terms, that element is the element of the conscious experience of God in human life. From the point of view of conscious experience, there could be no such thing without the work of the Spirit. The Spirit stands for the presence of God in human life working toward a divine purpose, especially for God's working in a conscious experience. The Spirit stands for God as making himself known in experience.

II

The Christian religion has two general aspects. These are both indispensable; and they are vitally related, yet distinguishable. These two phases or aspects are the historical and the experiential.

Christianity is not primarily a philosophy of life. Its facts and experiences are subject to philosophical treatment and interpretation.[1] In general terms, philosophy is a reasoned and systematic interpretation of life and its experiences. Christianity can

[1]Here is one place where I think Karl Barth and his followers miss the way. They have a philosophy of religion that says there can be no philosophy of religion.

be, at least with partial success, given a rational interpretation. But Christianity is more than a philosophy. It is a revelation from God; and any philosophical interpretation of Christianity must do justice to it as a revelation.

This revelation comes fundamentally in the person of Jesus Christ. He brings God in concrete, human, historical terms. Any interpretation of Christianity that is adequate must recognize that Christianity is a matter of history. God came to man in Jesus Christ. Of course, there was a long line of historical preparation in the general history of the world, and more specifically in the history of the Jewish people as recorded in the Old Testament. But all this led up to and culminated in the coming of Jesus of Nazareth. He stands for an objective, historical revelation of God.

Of course, there are other historical religions in the world. There are other religions that are founded religions. They go back to the life and work of individual men. Such was to some extent the Mosaic religion of the Old Testament. But Moses was not essential to Mosaism as Jesus Christ is to the Christian religion. This is expressed in John 1:17. John says that the law was given through Moses; grace and truth came through Jesus Christ. In the second clause of this statement, however, the word "came" does not adequately translate the Greek verb. What the author says is not that grace and truth *came* through Jesus Chirst, but that grace and truth *came to be* through him. It is the same verb that is used in John 1:3 when he says that all things *came to be* or were created through him. He is saying that grace and truth came into being, had their reality, were constituted, in and through him. These did not simply come into the world through him. They came into being through him. Grace and truth are not something God gives through him as an agent. He gives them in giving him.

Also, Mohammedanism, Buddhism, and Confucianism are founded religions. But none of these religions is identified with the person and work of its founder as Christianity is with Christ. These other religions, in each case, goes back to the teaching and work of its founder. But also in each case, the person of its founder is not essential to the religion as such. The religion can be something apart from the founder.[2] But in the case of Christianity the religion is nothing apart from Christ. Christianity is not a system of philosophy or theology, not a system of ethics, not a code of laws or conduct apart from Christ. Not only his teaching but his person is essential to his religion. Christianity is Christ, and Christ is Christianity. Christianity goes back to Christ and cannot be divorced from him.

III

This is something of what is meant by saying that the Christian religion is historical. But while Christ is historical, he is more than a character in and of history. He transcends history. He is super-historical. He is the eternal Christ come into history. He is the Jesus of history seen and apprehended as eternal Christ. This work of making the Jesus of history the eternal Christ is the counterpart of the incarnation in which the eternal

---

[2] Due to the emphasis on Mohammed as *The* prophet of the one God, he would come nearer being essential to Mohammedanism than Buddha and Confucius would be to the systems named for them.

Christ becomes the Jesus of history. According to Luke (1:31ff.) and Matthew (1:18ff.), it was through the Holy Spirit that the eternal Christ became incarnated as Jesus of Nazareth. On the other side, through death and resurrection, Jesus was glorified as the Christ of God. He became the universal, spiritual Christ instead of the local, limited Christ. And this universal, spiritual Christ is made real in the experiences of men through the work of the Holy Spirit. It is the work of the Spirit to reveal the universal, spiritual Christ to men of all races and climes. Without the Holy Spirit, this could not be.

Thus the Holy Spirit stands for the experiential element in the Christian religion. Christ is more than a figure in history who lived and died centuries ago. He can become the inner life of the soul. He does become the inner life of the soul that believes in him. Through the Spirit the crucified and risen Saviour is incarnated in those who believe in him. Without the Spirit Jesus would be only a historical character to men. But through him, Christianity is a living, transforming power in the life of men. More than that, Christ himself becomes a transforming power that works in the conscious experience of men. Through the work of the Spirit, our religion is one of conscious life and power. And this can be only in and through the Spirit. Paul says that no man can call Jesus Lord except in the Holy Spirit (1 Corinthians 12:3). Without the Spirit, our religion could not be a living experience. This is an indispensable element in our religion and it can only be through the Spirit. In a real sense, this is not simply a phase of our religion. This living experience is Christianity.

IV

We should consider this doctrine of the Spirit carefully because it has not been given proper treatment in the history of Christian thought. In early Christian history the doctrine of the person of Christ occupied the center of thought. Long and careful attention was given to that question. Just about all the possibilities were exhausted in the way of hypotheses to explain the facts. Of course, the forms of thought of that day were used. It could not be otherwise. The categories of thought used were mainly those of speculative Greek philosophy. But within the range of the forms of thought available at that time, the thinkers of that day gave thorough and exhaustive consideration to the doctrine of the person of Christ. Corresponding attention was not given to the doctrine of the Spirit. It was to be expected that the person of Christ should be given logical and temporal priority as compared with that of the Spirit. While both the historical and experiential factors in Christianity are essential, it was to be expected that the historical should be considered first. There are three doctrines in Christianity that are essentially related. These are the divinity of Christ, the personality of the Spirit, and the doctrine of the Trinity. Logically and temporally, they were developed in the order named.[3] In the New Testament the general order of treatment is first Christ and his work, then the Spirit and his work.[4] So it was not altogether a loss that the person of Christ should be treated first, but it was a loss that more attention was not given to the doctrine of the Spirit.

---

[3]Cf. my book, *Revelation and God*, pp. 327, 328.
[4]This will be treated more fully later.

Perhaps one reason the doctrine of the Spirit was not given more consideration in early Christian history following the apostolic era, as well as for centuries later, was that to its devotees Christianity was not so much a vital experience of the presence and transforming power of God as it was a system of doctrine or a matter of ecclesiastical conformity. This was unfortunate. In fact, it was a tragic loss. Nothing could make up for it. And it is inevitable that any form of Christianity that lacks a vital experience of the presence and power of God will give little attention to the doctrine of the Spirit. And it is worthy of note that this was not a case of knowing and emphasizing the historical Christ rather than the Spirit. It was rather a case of knowing neither. The historical and experiential factors are not rivals and mutually exclusive. They are rather mutually dependent and must go together. The fatal defect of the treatment of the person of Christ in early history was that it did not start from a knowledge of the Christ of the New Testament. It started rather from certain *a priori* assumptions and proceeded by way of abstract reasoning and thus necessarily arrived at defective conclusions. If the theologians who considered these matters had become more thoroughly acquainted with the life, character, and work of the Jesus Christ of the New Testament, they would have known better the Spirit and his work. They would consequently have been led to a more worthy view of the Spirit's nature and function. No man or group of men can have a proper insight into the doctrine of the Spirit who does not know his presence and power in human experience.

V

Another reason for giving a careful study to this doctrine is that it has been so badly perverted.

Some forms of Christianity have perverted the doctrine of God's working in human life by their sacramentalism and sacerdotalism. Any form of religion that makes the soul dependent on the observance of ordinances, ceremonies, or "sacraments," or the mediation of human priests for a knowledge of the grace of God in salvation is a perversion of New Testament Christianity. There is no such thing in the New Testament as a salvation that is mediated by priests or sacraments. The Lord's Supper and baptism may be considered as "means of grace" in the sense that they strengthen the faith of the participant who observes them as reminders of what Christ did for us in his death and resurrection. They may help to build up the faith of the participant. They also proclaim the gospel to observers. But they convey no saving grace; and there never has been a worse perversion of gospel truth than the the *ex opere operato* theory of the Catholic Church. The gospel is for those who can hear and appropriate its blessings by faith, and *only for them.*

There have been other types of Christianity of a more evangelical kind that have abused the doctrine of the Spirit. Catholicism rather confines the Spirit's work to the established and official procedures of the church. The real effect is to subject the work of the Spirit to the control of church dignitaries. It subordinates the divine to the control of man. It is religion controlled and subjected to human manipulation. There is an opposite type that gives us religion uncontrolled. It is religion of the spontaneous kind. It claims to seek for an exact reproduction of New Testament religion in letter and detail. It puts the emphasis on what seems to me to be incidentals associated with the work of the Spirit in the New Testament. One does not have the Spirit, we are told, unless he can talk in tongues, heal the sick miraculously and do things of that kind. Sometimes people of this type demonstrate their faith by letting rattlesnakes bite them and refuse doctors and all medical aid in sickness. Some religious bodies of this type claim a specific and instantaneous second work of grace in which the person is in some very definite sense made sinless. This strikes me as definitely fanatical and really discrediting to the doctrine of the Spirit and his work as set out in the New Testament.[5]

There are other perversions of the doctrine of the Spirit as bad as these mentioned above if not more so. One of these is Mormonism. Mormonism is as dogmatic as Roman Catholicism in its official claims of monopoly on the work of God among men and in its claim of right to dominion over mankind. It is also wild and fanatical in manifestations of the working of the Spirit. Such claims as those made by Catholicism, the modern holiness movements and Mormonism make all the more imperative a study of the whole question of the work of the Spirit in human life and religious experience.

VI

We should study the doctrine of the Spirit because of certain substitutes offered for the Spirit's work. Moving a little further off center, there are certain attitudes and movements that offer substitutes for

[5] I have discussed this and the Catholic doctrine further in a little book called *What Is a Saint?* published by the Broadman Press, Nashville, Tennessee.

the Spirit's work that make it important for us to understand the work of the divine Spirit. Some of these it might be difficult to class as to whether they are perversions of the doctrine or substitutes for the work of the Spirit. We will not try to make a hard and fast distinction here. But there are certain attitudes and movements—some of them within Christian ranks, some on the margin—that need consideration here.

Sometimes Christian workers may, and I think do, substitute high-powered emotionalism for the power of the Spirit. There are professional Christian workers, skilled in individual and mass psychology, who play upon human emotions to attain their ends. These are not always insincere and entirely unworthy people. But they play upon human emotions to secure apparent results in Christian character and life, and often these results are superficial and temporary. Some of these are engaged in evangelistic work, but not all. A superficial appeal to the emotions may be used in the field of education and other phases of religious activity as well as in evangelism. Some men have been quite successful in evangelism whose appeal was not mainly to the emotions.

One mistake often made, then, is to identify spirituality with an emotional type of religion. This is a serious error. Spirituality has to do with the whole man, not just with the emotions. Feeling has its legitimate place in religion, but it is by no means the whole of religion. I am not writing now with a reasoned theory of religion in mind like that of Schleiermacher, who identified religion with the feeling of dependence. I have in mind rather a popular attitude often expressed in such statements as, "I want a heart religion." What the speaker means is that he wants an emotional religion. But he is not aware of the fact that the Bible uses the word "heart" not for the emotions only but also for the whole inner life of man, including the mind. The Spirit of God has as much to do with man's mind as with his emotions. The idea that a preacher ought not to be educated or that he ought not to study to prepare for his next preaching appointment is based on the assumption (possibly often an unconscious assumption) that the Spirit has little or nothing to do with a man's mind. One of my early teachers used to say, "The Holy Spirit seems to have a strange affinity for a trained mind." A spiritual man is one who has the *mind* of the Lord. And the mind is closely linked with the conscience and the will. In fact, the Spirit has to do with the whole man. A man is not really a spiritual man unless the Spirit of God has control of the whole undivided personality. Another of my teachers used to say that emotion in religion is a dangerous thing unless kept under rational control.

An emotional religion, then, may not be a spiritual religion; it may be rather a substitute for spiritual power. One reason, no doubt, that some men resort to an emotional appeal in religion is because it is so much easier than dependence on divine power. The latter requires uprightness of character, patience in labor, surrender of selfish and sinful schemes, utter consecration to God and his will. A religion of spiritual power is costly. An emotional drive is much easier but also vastly less rewarding.

Another substitute for spiritual power is religious activism. There is a vast amount of activity carried on in some churches, and by individuals and groups outside the churches, that has little direct connection with the Spirit of God. Most, if not all, of this activity is good. Those who carry on the activity mean well and do much good. But what I am saying is that much of this activity is only remotely related to the direct guidance and power of the Spirit. There is a difference between doing the Lord's work under the guidance and power of the Holy Spirit and trying to do that work in the energy of the flesh. The Christian plan is that the followers of Jesus should not only do the Lord's work but that they should do that work under the direct guidance and power of the Spirit.

The New Testament justifies the belief that the Lord furnishes such direct guidance and power in doing his work. Here Jesus is our model. He sought always to know in detail what the Father's will for him was and he did that will in the power of the Spirit. It is not enough to seek to do good to one's fellows; that is good so far as it goes. But the Christian program of life includes doing the Father's will in the Power that he furnishes. Activity is not enough. Activity may be the activity of a galvanized corpse. Activity that is fully Christian is the activity of an individual or, more correctly, of a group possessed, guided, and empowered by the divine Spirit who indwells and empowers the Lord's people.

This is closely related to another very subtle danger—the danger of substituting organization for spiritual power. In the early days of Christian history there was the tendency to make up for the lack of spiritual power by developing ecclesiastical organization. As the spiritual fervor and power of New Testament days died out, ecclesiastical organization was developed. This was no accident. As spiritual power wanes, men feel the need of a substitute. They tend to substitute organization and the force of the impact of such organization for the dynamic of spiritual power.

The power of the Spirit gives freedom; the tendency of organization is to suppress freedom. The freedom of Christian men was gradually lost in the early centuries as the great Roman ecclesiastical machine grew. Organization is good, *provided* it is organization on Christian principles and informed and guided by the Spirit of God. Organization, if it is to be Christian, must be organization that expresses the spiritual freedom of Christian men. And I think I see some tendencies, very definite tendencies, to duplicate the process that took place in the early centuries—the process of substituting ecclesiastical organization for spiritual power and of suppressing spiritual power and freedom with organization. I think I see this tendency in some of the denominational activities today and in the high-pressure tendency to submerge the denominations in a great worldwide body. The danger here is the danger of developing another great Catholic Church after the order of the one centered in Rome.

Doubtless the advocates of organic church union will deny that they have anything of that kind in mind. That is readily granted. Neither did any one man or group of men plan what is now the Roman Catholic Church. Nevertheless, it came. Like Topsy, it "just growed." I used to hear Dr. George Burnam Foster describe how a certain movement in history took place. Then he would ask, "Who did it?" Then he would answer his own question by saying, "Nobody did it. It just did itself."

Such results never come into being full-grown. They grow gradually. They take time to grow. But they *do grow*. And, in my judgment, it is time that careful and prolonged attention be given to this movement toward church union. Men often quote the prayer of Jesus that his people be one, and then proceed on the assumption that he was praying for organic union. There is a vast difference between spiritual unity with full spiritual freedom and variety of organization on the one hand, and organic union where the impact of such an organic union is substituted for spiritual power and where freedom is suppressed. Unity in variety and variety in unity may be the sign of life; union and uniformity may be the sign of death.

It seems to me that back of some of the clamor today for church union is the assumption that the impact of a worldwide Christian organization would result in Christianizing the world at a much more rapid rate. Such an assumption is highly questionable. The impact of Christianity on the world is of a different order from that of big business or political pressure. Big business suppresses competition; therefore, men assume that, if the competition of the religious denominations could be eliminated, the impress of Christianity would be much more powerful. But big business seeks to destroy competition. Society has to be constantly on guard lest big business destroy competition and thereby destroy freedom. The inevitable tendency of a worldwide ecclesiastical organization would be to suppress freedom of thought and activity. There can be free co-operation for common ends among the varying religious bodies without the suppression of freedom. It is highly questionable whether the same freedom could be maintained in a world ecclesiastical organization. Whatever of co-operation among religious bodies there is to be, or of ecclesiastical organization, spiritual freedom and the principle of voluntary activity must be maintained if such co-operation or organization is to be Christian. And there is no use to sacrifice Christianity for the sake of effectiveness in Christian organization. Such effectiveness nullifies itself.

A pantheistic philosophy that identifies man and his powers with the divine is a practical denial of the work of the Holy Spirit. This substitutes the powers of man for the indwelling Spirit of God. While the Holy Spirit abides in man, it would not be the Christian view to identify the Holy Spirit with man's powers. It is true that Paul uses the word "spirit" in such a way in places that it is difficult to tell whether he is referring to the Spirit of God or the spirit of man.[6] It would doubtless be true to say that what Paul means by spirit in man includes man's capacity to receive the Spirit of God. Man, as a spiritual being, is capable of communion with the Spirit of God. Perhaps it would be more accurate to say that it is spirit in man that makes him capable of being taken up into fellowship with God through the creative activity of the Spirit of God in and on him. Yet it would not be true to Paul to identify man's powers with God or the Spirit of God.

In other words, spirituality is not to be identified with inwardness in religion. Here is another point where Catholic theology is rightfully subject to

---

[6] See for example Romans 8:11.

criticism. If one reads a book like *His Will Is Our Peace*, by Gerald Vann,[7] he will find much that is helpful to any Christian. Yet at the same time he will be conscious of a subtle, almost indefinable, difference between the type of piety inculcated in this book and that found in evangelical Christianity. The root principle in Mr. Vann's book, the principle out of which grace is to grow, is love—love to God and man. But it is love which the Christian is to cultivate. The Christian's peace is thus dependent on something that the Christian is to do—a state of character and mind that he is to produce. Mr. Vann tells us that no torments can overcome one's peace if his love is *great enough and strong enough.* The Christian's peace, then, depends on his producing in himself a love strong enough to consume all opposition. Thus, in the last analysis, one's peace depends on something that he is to do—which really means that he will have no permanent, abiding peace.

Over against this, evangelical Christianity makes love something shed abroad in our hearts by the Holy Spirit given to us. Mr. Vann makes love cultivated in one's heart by oneself the root principle of the Christian life; Paul makes faith the root principle and love the fruit. And the virtue of faith, as Paul teaches, is found not in faith as a subjective principle, but faith as apprehending Christ and the grace of God. Man's inner musings or broodings are not the same as spirituality. Subjectivity is not spirituality. The Spirit of God is other than man and in that sense entirely objective to man. One of the dangers of the doctrine of the Spirit in the case of some people is that they may identify their mus-

---

[7]Published by Sheed & Ward, N. Y., 1947.

ings or impressions or even their own hallucinations with the voice of God. One test to be applied here is the moral test. Spirit in the Bible is always a moral concept. In the Bible, the word "spirit" always carries a moral connotation, and nothing immoral can be attributed to the Spirit of God.[8]

In current usage sometimes the esthetic, the refined, the cultural, are spoken of as spiritual. One would not care to deny that the Spirit of God, in the more general sense of the term, has anything to do with the beautiful and the refined. But this would hardly be using the word spiritual in the New Testament sense. The Spirit of God in the New Testament is distinctly the *Holy* Spirit —holy in character himself and seeking to produce holiness in man. A high type of humanistic religion could put emphasis on the refined and the beautiful and speak of these as spiritual. But this type of religion can also deny man's dependence on God and neglect, if not deny, the distinctive work of the Spirit as understood in evangelical Christianity.

[8]This thought will be developed further later.

CHAPTER II

THE SPIRIT IN THE OLD TESTAMENT

I

There are two types of religion in the Old Testament. One is the type represented by the law of Moses, written on tables of stone. The law was given through Moses as an agent or representative of God. It was written on tables of stone and administered by priests whose priesthood came from the fact that they were descendants of other priests. These priests were officials in a state that was regarded as having Jehovah as its King. No moral or spiritul qualifications were required of these priests for holding their position as priests or for administering their official duties. It is true that there were at times elaborate ceremonial cleansings required of these priests. These were required as a condition of entering upon their official duties or of performing these duties. These cleansings were no doubt symbolical of holiness, but holiness was not necessarily moral in nature in legal religion. The religion represented by the priests and the law was legalistic, racial, external, institutional. The Spirit may deal with individuals in such a system, but spirituality will not characterize such a system as a whole. Official priests in any religion have never been noted for spirituality in a moral sense.

Along with this legal and institutional form of religion in the Old Testament there was another of a different type. These two types are not entirely exclusive of each other, but they are antithetical in character. This second type might be described as spiritual, personal, and prophetic in character. Moses was a representative of this type as well as of the institutional type. This is due to the fact that Moses was both a prophet and the founder of the legal system of the Old Testament. As indicated above, there could be, even in a legal system, individuals who enjoyed a spiritual and prophetic type of experience.

The leaders of this second type of religion, the prophets, did not hold any official position in the established religious system of national Israel. They were not officials either by heredity or by any kind of civil or ecclesiastical appointment. They were leaders in religion by virtue of a divine call and did their work by the force of personal leadership and moral and spiritual influence. They stood for a type of religion that was moral and mystical in character. As a rule they were the critics of the established order of things, both in religion and state. They spent much of their time and effort in denouncing the failures and corruption of the priestly class and the civil authorities of the day. Naturally this was an irksome task. These men often felt their call and commission as a "burden" from the Lord (Isaiah 14:28; 16:1; 17:1; 22:1; 23:1, ASV with margin). This criticism of the *status quo* often led to the persecution and even to the death of the prophets. Established religion rarely appreciates the criticism of free lancers.

I spoke of this type of religion as mystical. By this I mean that it stands for the direct access of the individual soul into the presence of God and the experience by the individual of indwelling presence of God. Of course this feature of religion is not realized in fulness until we get to the New Testament; but we have the roots of it in the Old. It breaks out occasionally even in the most legalistic portions of the Old Testament, but it is best represented in the Psalms and the Prophets. The classic expression of such religion is still found in the writings of the prophets and in such Psalms as the twenty-third, the thirty-fourth, the fifty-first, and many others.

Jesus built on this prophetic type of religion. He brought it to its climax and finality. He fulfilled the Law and the Prophets, the whole Old Testament system. By bringing prophetic religion to its finality, by opening the way for every soul of man to have direct access to the Father in the Spirit (Ephesians 2:18), he fulfilled the prophets. He also fulfilled the legal system of the Old Testament. He fulfilled the Prophets and Psalms by making it possible for all men to enjoy to the full the fellowship with God that, to some extent, the psalmists and prophets of the Old Testament enjoyed. We have in Christian experience the noonday sun, whereas they had the day dawn. He fulfilled the legal system of the Old Testament in another sense. He made possible for us that access to God which the law symbolized and foreshadowed but could not make real. This is expressed in the book of Hebrews in the New Testament. The law with its types and shadows could not bring to man the reality; the reality came in Christ. And when the reality came, the types and shadows passed away. Thus the priestly type of religion was fulfilled in Christ and abolished.

The prophetic type was fulfilled in being completed and made permanent.

II

The word translated "spirit" in the Old Testament (Hebrew, *"ruach"*) means breath, wind, spirit. As the breath of man or animal, the *ruach* was the life principle in him (or it). When the *ruach* departed, he was dead. When God breathed into man's nostrils the breath of life, man became a living soul (Genesis 2:7). Man's body was composed of flesh. His flesh animated by his spirit constituted him a living soul.

Spirit stands for invisible energy or power. The Spirit of God is the outgoing energy or power of God working in the world. This energy or power is not thought of as something apart from God, yet it is, at least in places, spoken of as something distinct from him. It would seem that the Spirit of God is thought of after the analogy of the spirit of man as something that belongs to God. Nowhere in the Old Testament do we have exactly the conception attributed to Jesus (John 4:24) that God is spirit. But we do have the Spirit of God conceived as the outgoing energy or power of God. This outgoing energy or power of God must not be thought of, however, as something apart from God himself. This power does not exist apart from God. Rather should it be thought of as God's own presence or power. In places the Spirit is specifically made synonymous with the presence of God, as in Psalm 139:7, where the writer asks, "Whither shall I go from thy spirit? or whither shall I flee from thy presence?" In the next verse, the author says that if he ascends into heaven, God is there; or if he makes his bed in hell (Sheol), behold, God is there. He is expressing the impossibility of getting away from God. He is omnipresent. The thing that makes it possible for him to be omnipresent is that he is a spiritual Being. He is present or omnipresent in his Spirit.

The Spirit of God is God himself immanent in the world or in human life. Not only does the Spirit stand for God as present or immanent in the world or man, but also as energizing—energizing to effect a purpose of God. The doctrine of the Spirit in the Old Testament prevents the conception of God from becoming wholly transcendent. The God of the Old Testament is transcendent, but the Spirit brings him down into the realm of creation and makes him real and active in creation and more particularly in man.

The idea of spirit as power is set out in a contrast expressed in Isaiah 31:1-3. The prophet is rebuking those who look to Egypt and her military might for safety rather than to Jehovah. He says that the Egyptians are men and not God. Their horses are flesh and not spirit. Man in his weakness and blindness is set in contrast to Jehovah in his wisdom and might, while horses as flesh are set in contrast to the invisible but real power of spirit. We have something of the same contrast in Zechariah 4:6 where the message comes to Zerubbabel, saying: "Not by might [an army], nor by power, but my Spirit, saith the Lord of hosts." Man and flesh stand for weakness and failure; God and his Spirit stand for real power and success.

The Old Testament thus represents the Spirit as operative in nature and bestowing extraordinary powers on man in what we ordinarily think of as his natural life. This is in line with Old Testament monotheism which conceived of the world order and man's powers as all being the creation of God and as being sustained by him. So in Genesis 1:2,[1] we find that the Spirit of God moved (or brooded) over the face of the waters in a world that was waste and void and where darkness covered the face of the deep. The suggestion is that the Spirit was the power to bring order out of chaos and light out of darkness. In Job 26:13, Job says that by his (God's) Spirit the heavens are garnished.[2]

As to man and his powers, it is said in Genesis 2:7 that Jehovah God formed man of the dust of the ground and breathed (a verb expressing an idea closely related to the noun *"ruach"*, spirit) into man's nostrils the breath of life and man became a living soul. The idea seems to be that God inspirited man and thus gave him life or made him a living being. Again Job says (27:3) that his life is yet (after all that he has suffered) whole within him and the Spirit of God is in his nostrils. The Spirit of God could refer to the divine Spirit as producing life in Job or Job's spirit or breath as God's work in him (Job). In 33:4, we hear Elihu saying that the Spirit of God had made him, and the breath of the Almighty gives him life. The life of man is thus recognized as God's gift produced in man by his Spirit.

III

We have a number of passages in the Old Testament in which special powers are bestowed on man by the divine Spirit. These powers belong to what

---

[2]This too may refer to the action of a sudden and brisk wind that swept away the fog and clouds and brought clear skies.

[1]Could the word *"ruach"* here mean wind and suggest that a divinely-sent wind brought these beneficent results?

we call the natural realm. They are supernatural, however, in the sense that they are the gifts of God. They are bestowed by the Spirit. They are not man's attainments; God gives them. Another thing to remember is that these gifts are bestowed for a divine purpose or end. They are not bestowed primarily for the sake of the one on whom they are bestowed. The purpose is usually, if not always, theocratic; that is, given for the sake of advancing God's control and direction of Israel as God's chosen people. These gifts were gracious in the sense that the recipients did not earn or deserve them and were given for God's ends, not those of a private individual.

Some examples of the bestowment of these supernatural gifts in the natural realm are as follows:

There is the case of Bezaleel and his associates (Exodus 31:3ff. and 35:30ff.). Bezaleel was filled with the Spirit so that he had wisdom, understanding, and knowledge in all kinds of workmanship. Notice also that this skill and knowledge were given to Aholiab and others associated with Bezaleel in this enterprise. Others were given the skill necessary to carry out the enterprise which was God's, not theirs. These men were endowed not for their sakes but for the sake of Israel and the accomplishment of God's purpose. The Spirit came upon Samson and he was given extraordinary physical strength (Judges 14:6). Jephthah's military skill resulted from the fact that the Spirit came upon him (Judges 11:29ff.). After a period of providential preparation, the Spirit of God came upon Gideon and he led Israel to victory (Judges 6:34 and context). Each of these men who were thus endowed by the Spirit was a more or less direct representative of Israel as God's chosen people.

There is nothing surprising in the fact that these natural gifts are represented as the supernatural bestowment of God if we keep in mind that man is God's creature and that all man's powers come from God. As these men in this situation used their powers to carry forward the purpose of God in Israel, so should all men devote all their powers to God and his service. Man's sin has consisted in the fact that he used his God-given powers for selfish and ignoble ends.

So far as I recall, we do not have in the New Testament a similar representation of the life and powers of man as the direct gift of the divine Spirit or of the Spirit's working in the natural realm. In one place Paul seems to give something of a cosmic reference to the Spirit's operation. I think it is a fair inference from what Paul says in Romans 8:22 and context that the indwelling Spirit is thought of as the power that creates a (poetic) longing in nature for deliverance from evil and corruption and that the Spirit is the power that will effect this desired consummation.

IV

The main work of the divine Spirit in the Old Testament was in the spiritual realm. Several phases of this we will consider. One of these is in the work of the prophets. We have already noticed the difference between priestly and prophetic religion in the Old Testament. Priestly religion is the religion of human or priestly manipulation. It is based on the principle that man can control and direct divine power for man's benefit. Old Testament religion, it is true, based this on the assumption that God had instituted the system in which this was done. But, nevertheless, it goes on the idea of human control of God's power. Prophetic religion is the opposite of this. Prophetic religion was one of divine initiative and divine sovereignty. It sought to bring about divine control of man's life, individual and collective. The prophets were called of God (1 Samuel 3:1-9; 1 Kings 17:2; Isaiah 1:1; 6:1ff.; Jeremiah 1:1, etc.). They received their message from God (Isaiah 1:1; Jeremiah 1:1, etc.). They spoke in the name of God. They denounced those who came in their own name or brought their own dreams as a message from God (Ezekiel 13:3ff.).

In the early days of Old Testament history prophecy was not on a very high level. Sometimes the prophet acted in a fantastic and almost irresponsible manner. See the instances of Saul and his servants and of Balaam (1 Samuel 10:10ff.; 1 Samuel 19:18ff.; Numbers 22:5ff.). We see something corresponding to this in what appears to be ecstatic experiences and the glossolalia of the New Testament, especially at Corinth as reflected in 1 Corinthians 12-14. Paul distinctly discourages these lower manifestations of the Spirit's work and puts the emphasis on the ethical and higher spiritual qualities. The subjects of Old Testament prophecy were not always on a high moral and spiritual level, as seen in Saul's seeking his father's asses (1 Samuel 10:14ff.). Hunting animals of an assinine variety is not the highest occupation for a Spirit-called and Spirit-endued prophet. But as religion became ethicized, as the conception of God became more moral, the work of the prophets became correspondingly elevated. The result is that in the religion led and largely produced by the prophets and prophetic class of religious leaders, we have the highest type of religion known to the world except that founded by Jesus.

In Numbers 11:25ff. we have an account that makes it clear that the thing that constituted a man a prophet was the fact that God put his Spirit in the man. The seventy that were chosen as assistants to Moses were made prophets when the Lord took of the Spirit that was on Moses and put this Spirit on these men.

Sometimes the power of prophecy seems to have been a temporary gift—one might almost say a seizure by the Spirit, as in the cases of Saul and his servants. Nor did prophesying in some cases seem to have any essential relation to spiritual character in the prophet. But in the great prophets like Samuel, Elijah, and later on Isaiah, Jeremiah, and others it certainly was a permanent calling. In many instances, too, as with Samuel, there was a clear, providential preparation for this work, and God so dealt with the prophet in preparing him for this work as to make him a representative of God not only in word but also in character and life. Also, these prophets were not simply foretellers of the future; they were *forthtellers* for God. They interpreted, under the Spirit's leading, God's will for their day, and thus largely for all times. They set out, first of all for their day, the great moral and spiritual principles on which God deals with men. In doing this, their messages come to have a permanent significance for all times and for all men.

V

One phase of the Spirit's work as represented in the Old Testament is with reference to the coming Messiah. Most of the material on this point comes from the prophets. In the Old Testament, we find men being anointed as prophets,[3] priests, and kings. The anointing was a ceremony in which oil was poured on one's head, usually by a prophet. Whatever else this ceremony represented, it signified that the one being anointed was being set aside for a work for Jehovah the God of Israel. And the pouring of the oil on his head probably signified the qualifying of the anointed one by Jehovah for his work. Whether understood at the time or not, the ultimate fulfilment was in the coming of the Spirit on men to qualify them for God's service. The significance in relation to the Spirit is made clear in a passage like 1 Samuel 16:13. Samuel anoints David king of Israel and immediately it is said that the Spirit of Jehovah came on him mightily from that day forward. Even Saul was given qualifications from God to rule Israel until he completely forfeited the divine favor by a rebellious spirit.

We also find in the Old Testament One to whom the writers looked forward, who was to be God's anointed in a special sense. In various ways and under different forms, reference is made to this coming Deliverer of God's people. It may be quite impossible for us always clearly to identify this Coming One and distinguish him from other figures in the Old Testament. Fortunately, this is not necessary for our purpose. It is made clear from certain Old Testament statements, particularly if we may be

---

[3]Some scholars would question this statement as applied to prophets.

permitted to interpret some of them in the light of the New Testament, that the Holy Spirit was to qualify this Coming One for his divine mission.

Certain passages about which we might not be entirely clear as to their direct messianic reference include 1 Samuel 2:10, where Jehovah is to exalt the horn of his anointed; Psalms 2:2, where the rulers take counsel against Jehovah and his anointed. There are others where the reference to the coming Messiah (especially in view of the New Testament statements) are more certain. One of the first to come to mind is Isaiah 11:2. A shoot from the stock of Jesse is to come forth and a branch from his roots bear fruit. The Spirit of Jehovah will rest upon him, and he will have all the qualities necessary to rule. This Spirit of Jehovah on him is to be a spirit of wisdom and understanding, of counsel and might, of knowledge, and of the fear of Jehovah. He is to judge and rule with patience, grace and righteousness.

In Isaiah 40-66, there appears the figure of the Servant of the Lord with whom Jesus identified himself. In 42:1, Jehovah is represented as saying, "I have put my Spirit upon him." Then, evidently as a result of having the Spirit, his qualities for carrying out his divine mission are set out. In 59:21, Jehovah speaks and says, "My Spirit that is upon thee." In 61:1, we have the statement, "The Spirit of the Lord is upon me; because he hath anointed me to preach good tidings unto the meek." His mission is then described in terms of the year of Jubilee. In Luke 4:16ff., we find Jesus claiming that this passage is being fulfilled in himself, and his mission is described in the terms found in Isaiah's prophecy.

So we see the Old Testament writers saying that
the Son of David, or the Servant of Jehovah, will be
anointed with the Spirit to qualify him for his messianic mission, and then we find the New Testament
telling us that these predictions have been fulfilled in
Jesus, upon whom the Spirit came at his baptism
and who did all his works in the power of the
Spirit of God.

VI

We have some material in the Old Testament dealing with the work of the Spirit in the life of the
individual worshipper. It would be difficult to draw
a line of distinction between this and what was said
about the Spirit's work in the life of the prophets.
In fact, what the Spirit did for the prophets is an
example of the nature of the work that the Spirit
may do in and for the individual. There is this
difference, however. When the Spirit's call made
one a prophet, he became more than a private
individual; he to some extent became a representative
of public or social religion. The prophet was an
individual, but when he became a prophet he became a representative of God to other men. As a
prophet he was concerned not only with his own
relation with God; he became one who by virtue
of his being a prophet was concerned with the
standing of other men before God. He became
concerned with their receiving God's blessings and
performing their duties toward God. If we might
be allowed a distinction where absolute separation
is out of the question, as an individual a man deals
with God and God deals with him on his own account
and for his own sake, while as a prophet God deals
with him as a representative of others. But in
either phase of the prophet's experience, we would

have revealed to us something of the Spirit's dealings with one as an individual religious man and
of man's capacities to receive and respond to God's
dealings with him.

There is no better place to see what the Spirit
means to the individual than in some of the psalms.
We have already referred to Psalm 139:7. Here in
parallel lines the Spirit of God and the presence of
God are set forth as synonymous. Observing the
context in this psalm, I take it that the Spirit stands
for two things. One is the presence of God; the
other is God's searching knowledge of man. The
writer recognizes that he cannot get away from
the presence of God. In life or death, he is beset
with God's presence. In earth, or heaven, or Sheol,
he is confronted with God. In his Spirit God is
omnipresent. Not only is God present, he judges,
searches, tries man. Man is known of God, and
in being known he is also searched and judged.

Another passage bearing on the work of the Spirit
in the life of the individual is found in Psalm 51:
10-11. This passage is set in a context of intense
personal religion. The psalmist confesses his sin
and pleads for mercy. He asks for forgiveness and
cleansing. He makes an intensely personal confession of sin and prays that God will wash him clean
and restore the joy of salvation. When he prays (v.
11) that the Lord will not cast him from his (the
Lord's) presence nor take his Holy Spirit away from
him, we see the Holy Spirit and the Lord's presence
again used as synonymous. It is clear that the presence of the Holy Spirit means cleansing, restoration,
joy, and usefulness. With sins forgiven, heart
cleansed, the joy of salvation restored, the Holy
Spirit abiding with him, he will teach transgressors

the ways of God and sinners will be converted to God. We have something of the same thing here that we have in the New Testament. The Holy Spirit, making real the presence of God, produces confession, cleansing, joy, and usefulness. This is one of only three instances in the Old Testament where the Spirit of God is called the Holy Spirit. It may be worth noting that in each case the context is one in which the character of God is represented as redemptive. Here in Psalm 51 he is One who cleanses, heals, and restores the backslidden individual. The other references (Isaiah 63:10-11) present him as the Redeemer of the house of Israel. This is in line with Old Testament thought that Jehovah as the Holy One of Israel is the Redeemer of his people (Isaiah 41:14; 43:14).

VII

Another thing that we have in the Old Testament is the promise of a future age when the Spirit will be with and in all God's people.

In Jeremiah 31:31ff., we have the promise of a time coming when the Lord will make a new covenant with his people. He will no longer write his law upon tables of stone but in their hearts and upon their minds. A knowledge of his will will be written in the inward parts of his people, so that all the Lord's people will have a knowledge of God and it will no longer be necessary for them to teach every one his neighbor saying, "Know the Lord," for they shall each and all know him, from the least to the greatest. We have practically the same thing in Jeremiah 32:35ff. and in Ezekial 11:19-21. Here we have set in contrast the two types of religion spoken of at the beginning of this chapter. One is the religion of the law which was written on tables of stone. Over against this the prophets envision a time when a knowledge of God and his will will be written on the inner nature of man. A knowledge of God will then be a matter of spiritual experience. It is to be noted that in these passages we have that oft-recurring statement that Jehovah will be their God, and those who have this inner, personal knowledge of God will be his people. In the Old Testament, God's people were a redeemed people. Israel became God's people by being redeemed with the mighty hand of Jehovah from Egypt. Now the prophets see that a time is coming when God's people will be those who are made his by a spiritual redemption—one that gives to each individual man a direct and personal knowledge of God. Here we are getting close to the ideal of religion realized in the New Testament.

We have another passage (Joel 2:28ff.) in which the prophet says that the day is coming when the Lord will pour out his Spirit upon all flesh. The language following indicates that the Spirit is to be the possession of all God's people. Old and young, male and female, slaves and free people are all to have this great power bestowed on them. On the day of Pentecost, Peter interprets what is there happening as the fulfilment of this prophecy. Old Testament religion was one in which the Spirit of God as a direct and conscious experience was limited to only a select few of God's people. The New Testament gives us a religion in which this conscious possession of the Spirit is the birthright of all God's redeemed children.

CHAPTER III

THE HOLY SPIRIT IN THE SYNOPTICS

In general we do not find this doctrine in developed form in the Synoptics. The doctrine is rather elementary as compared with the rest of the New Testament. This is not due to the date of their writing, because these Gospels are later than some other writings in the New Testament that have a more fully developed doctrine of the Spirit. This is specifically true of some of the Epistles of Paul. First Corinthians and Romans were almost certainly written before these Gospels, but they have a more mature doctrine of the Spirit than do these Gospels. This more elementary doctrine of the Spirit in the Synoptics must be due to the fact that they are historically reliable in reflecting the situation which they claim to tell about, namely, the situation during the earthly life of Jesus rather than the situation at the date of their final composition as we now have them. This would not fit in very well with the idea of some "form" critics of today who claim that these Gospels reflect the situation at the date of their composition rather than the situation in the days of Jesus.

Another fact that soon becomes evident as we read these Gospels is that Luke gives a fuller account of the activity of the Spirit during the life of Jesus than do Matthew and Mark. Mark's account of the work of the Spirit is quite sparse, and Matthew's account is not much fuller. Luke gives considerably more attention to the matter but not so much as John and Paul. Of course, Luke gives much more attention to the work of the Spirit in Acts. I have nothing very definite to offer as an explanation of the fact that Luke in the Gospel treats this matter more fully than do Mark and Matthew. We might observe, however, that this is not out of harmony with the emphasis of Luke on the gracious character of God and of Jesus as we see this aspect of the divine manifestation in Luke. In answer to the charge that he was friendly with publicans and sinners, Jesus defends himself by portraying God as being merciful to the lost and wandering sons of men (Luke 15). It is not out of line with this that Luke represents God in this book as sending out his Spirit to work in the hearts and lives of men and bring them into harmony with himself in his gracious activity among men. Besides, Luke's familiarity with the work of the Spirit, as it is set forth in Acts and as he came in contact with the Spirit's activity in the work of Paul, might help to explain his sensitivity to the manifestations of the Spirit during the earthly life of Jesus.

I

We have a whole series of manifestations of the working of the divine Spirit in the first and second chapters of Luke. These are not given by the other Synoptic writers with the exception of what Matthew has to say about the virgin birth of Jesus. This series of manifestations of the Spirit has to do with what Luke portrays as prophetic insight into the coming birth and work of Jesus as Messiah. This prophetic insight was manifested by a number of devout Jews whose hearts the Lord had evidently prepared for this very purpose; namely, that they should see and bear witness to the meaning of what was taking place in their midst. John the Baptist, of course, as *the* forerunner of Jesus, was the main one of those to whom God gave prophetic insight, but there were a number of others as well.

One of these others was Elizabeth upon the occasion of her visit with Mary. She was filled with the Holy Spirit and lifted up her voice and pronounced a blessing on Mary (Luke 1:41-45). To this Mary responded in what is usually called the Magnificat in Luke 1:46-55. Another instance is that of Zacharias. We are told that he was filled with the Holy Spirit and prophesied. His prophecy is recorded in Luke 1:68-79. The occasion was the birth and naming of John the Baptist. He seems to have been given insight into the meaning of what God was doing for his people. He had at least some understanding of the nature and scope of the salvation that God was bringing to men. The Holy Spirit also came upon Simeon. It had been revealed to him by the Spirit that he should not die until he had seen the Lord's Christ. When he saw Jesus as an infant, Simeon seemed to recognize him as the Christ and the bringer of salvation to Israel. He seemed also to recognize the scope of this salvation as including more than the Jews (Luke 2:22-32).

In these instances we have something like the prophetic inspiration of the Old Testament. Sometimes prophetic inspiration in the Old Testament seemed to have been a temporary matter. (See the case of Saul, 1 Samuel 10:9-13). In other instances it was more a permanent matter as in the case of prophets like Samuel, Jeremiah, Isaiah, and Ezekiel. In the case of these forerunners of Jesus it was more of a temporary matter as it was in some other New Testament cases later. (See Acts 21:7-14.) But in the case of these people we are considering, it was evidently a special gift that came to people who were upright and genuinely religious.

There was one forerunner of Jesus, however, who stood out above all the others. When a forerunner of Jesus is mentioned, everyone would think immediately of John the Baptist. Some of these characters to whom Luke gives considerable space in his first two chapters are brought into the account because of their relation to John. That would apply, of course, particularly to Zacharias and Elizabeth.

In reference to John there is a rather unusual statement made about him in Luke 1:15. He was to abstain from strong drink like an Old Testament Nazirite (separated one, Numbers 6:3), and should be filled with the Holy Spirit from his mother's womb. Whatever else this meant, it meant that his life in a special way was to be under the control of God from the beginning and was to be dedicated to God.

John was also in the desert until the time of his showing forth to Israel (Luke 1:80). Here Luke tells us that he grew and waxed strong in spirit. His inner life developed as he had fellowship with God in the solitary places. The Holy Spirit does not have much of a chance at men in the mad rush and whirl of things in the life of the modern world. Solitude is essential for growing strong Christian character. It might be too strong to say that physical solitude is an absolute essential, but at least mental and spiritual solitude are; and it is very difficult to secure these without some measure of physical solitude. One woman told me that she found perfect peace of mind and soul by seeking God in a crowded place of work; but hers was an exceptional case. Most of us do not have the strength of mind and concentration of desire and purpose to secure spiritual solitude without the aid of physical solitude. The solitary places have been the habitat of strong spiritual characters. Jesus went to the solitary places to pray.

Luke gives us a quite formal and dignified announcement of the coming of the Word of God to John (3:1-2). From the way Luke locates the event in relation to the reigning Caesar in the empire and to the governors of surrounding provinces and to the high priesthood in Judea, one gets the impression that he is announcing an event of great importance. No doubt that is the impression Luke means to give. He seems to be building up to a climax. After carefully locating the event in relation to current history, it might seem an anticlimax simply to say that "the word of God came to John, son of Zacharias in the wilderness." But was it an anticlimax? Indeed, it was not. It was an event of great significance for Israel and for the world when the Word of God came to John in the wilderness. A new day was breaking for the people of God. The voice of prophecy had been silent in Israel now for a long period. But that voice is about to be heard again.

There is a close association in the Bible between the Word of God and the Spirit of God. Paul speaks of the sword of the Spirit which is the Word of God (Ephesians 6:17). I take it that he means that the Word of God is the weapon that the Spirit uses in fighting the battles of the Lord. We might say that between the Word of God and the Spirit there is a double relationship. One is that the Spirit produces the Word. The Spirit is the agent or power that brings to men God's message embodied in his Word. The other relationship is that the Spirit uses the Word as just indicated.

So we find the Word of God coming to John who was filled with the Spirit from his mother's womb. Following the statement that the Word of God came to John, we find him preaching a baptism of repentance unto (or into) the remission of sins. His baptism was one that symbolized the passage of the one baptized into a state or condition of remission of sins. John preached essentially the same message that Jesus did. They both came proclaiming that the Kingdom was at hand and calling on men to change their minds and be ready for the reign of God (Matthew 3:1-2; Mark 1:14-15). John came to prepare the way for the coming King. The King's highway must be made ready. The hills must be brought low, the valleys filled in, and the crooked places made straight.

Many writers have emphasized the aspect of sternness and judgment in John's preaching. That element is there. He said that the ax was laid at the root of the trees, and every tree that did not bring forth good fruit was to be hewn down and cast into the fire (Luke 3:9). But it is also to be stated that John said that, while he was to baptize in water, the One coming after him should baptize in the Holy Spirit (Mark 1:8; Luke 3:16). John seems, then, to be getting a glimpse of the fact that the One whom he was introducing to Israel was to usher in a spiritual order or reign.

John not only demanded repentance of the people, but also that they should bring forth fruits worthy of repentance (Luke 3:8). Natural descent from Abraham was not sufficient. Spiritual character cannot be inherited. That which is born of the flesh is flesh. John demanded of those that he baptized that they manifest a changed mind by a changed life. Luke 3:9-14 shows that John knew the people of his day. He knew their sins and failures, and he demanded of each group evidence fitting their situation that they had repented.

John's ministry, then, manifested a spiritual quality of a high order. It was not, of course, on a par with that of Jesus, but it was an effective preparation for that of Jesus. He made ready a people prepared for the Lord.

There is one instance in the Synoptics of a reference to the work of the Spirit in the Old Testament. The account is given in Mark 12:35-37, with the parallels in Matthew and Luke. Jesus says that David in the Holy Spirit called the Messiah Lord. This means, no doubt, that David wrote this under the control of the Holy Spirit and is a distinct recognition of the guidance of the Spirit in the writing of Old Testament Scripture. It is a little surprising that we find in these Gospels as little as we do on the work of the Spirit in Old Testament times.

II

It is also surprising that we find no more than we do about the Spirit in relation to the disciples of Jesus.

Taking the account as a whole, in line with specific statements in other places in the New Testament, I think we can affirm that the recognition of Jesus as Messiah on the part of the disciples was the result of spiritual enlightenment. I do not recall any place in these Gospels where their perception of his Messiahship is directly attributed to the Holy Spirit. We do have later Paul's statement that no man can call Jesus Lord except in the Holy Spirit (1 Corinthians 12:3). And we have the statement attributed to Jesus that flesh and blood had not revealed to Peter that Jesus was Messiah, but that the Father had revealed it to him (Matthew 16:17). What God does in the inner life of man he does through his Spirit.

That Jesus was the Christ seems to have been the original Christian confession. When Peter confesses Jesus as the Christ, Jesus welcomes the confession and accepts it, which was a virtual affirmation of it on his part. And when Peter (speaking for the group) makes this confession, Jesus in substance says that it is not a human discovery that is being brought to light but a divine revelation that is being stated. God was working in the minds and hearts of men to bring them to see the significance of the person and work of Jesus.

Another evidence of the work of the Spirit set forth in the Synoptics is seen in the qualities required of the Kingdom. Jesus required childlikeness of those who would be his disciples. They must have the qualities of humility, obedience, teachableness. Sometimes men have seemed to think that in his teaching Jesus was encouraging men to recognize in themselves their native godlikeness and to seek to develop themselves into good citizens of the Kingdom. The Sermon on the Mount, we have been told, did not recognize any need for atonement, regeneration, and a supernatural salvation. But such a view comes from a superficial reading.

In John Jesus is represented as saying to Nicodemus that one must be born again to see or enter the kingdom of God. While not stated in just that way, the same truth lies embedded in the Sermon on the Mount.

There Jesus says that the meek, the poor in spirit, the peacemakers, are the blessed ones. They are the ones who are the sons of God, and the ones to whom belongs the kingdom of heaven. He says that unless men have a righteousness that exceeds that of the scribes and Pharisees, they cannot enter the Kingdom. The righteousness of the scribes and Pharisees was external, legalistic, measurable by the yardstick. Those entering the Kingdom must have a righteousness that is internal, spiritual, personal. They must be above external acts of murder and sexual immorality because their hearts are pure from those things. They will be like their Father in heaven. They will have good will toward all men, even their enemies and those who persecute and despitefully use them. Now if a man does not see that this calls for a change of heart on the part of men as they are by nature, there is not much use to try to show it to him. It means exactly what Jesus said in John: "Ye must be born again" (John 3:7). That is the work of the Spirit.

Jesus promises the Holy Spirit to his disciples when they are called on to defend themselves before persecuting authorities (Matthew 10:20. cf. Mark 13:11; Luke 12:11-12). The three Gospels set this promise in different contexts, but in essence it is the same. In each case the disciples are being tried before hostile authorities for preaching the gospel. He tells them not to be anxious beforehand as to what they shall say, for the Holy Spirit

(Spirit of your Father, Matthew says) will give them what they shall say.

I take it that it is hardly necessary to say that it is a perversion of this passage to make it a counsel of universal application in regard to public address on behalf of Christ and his cause. Some have made it a rule applicable to Christian preaching—even a rule against ministerial education. We have been told that the education of a preacher was shutting out the Holy Spirit and that a preacher should not prepare beforehand a sermon, but let the Lord give him his message as he delivers it. One thing I have observed is that a little thought beforehand seemed to prevent a lot of aimless wandering while one is speaking. Jesus gives this assurance only with reference to defense before a hostile and persecuting authority, and we are responsible for any extension of it beyond that. The Lord did not apply it so.

Those who have thus misapplied this promise of Jesus have evidently had a false assumption underlying their reasoning. They have reasoned on the assumption that the Holy Spirit has to do only with the spontaneous in religion. Undoubtedly the divine Spirit has often been the power operative in the spontaneous in man's religious life. But to assume that the Holy Spirit has to do only with the spontaneous would be putting too much of a limitation on the Lord in regard to this matter. Why cannot God work in and through the mind of a devout and prayerful minister as he studies and plans for next Sunday's service as well as through his feelings and thoughts after he gets in the pulpit on Sunday morning? As a rule, if the Spirit has not guided as the minister prepares during the week, it is doubtful whether he will have much place in the service during its process. Certainly this promise of Jesus to his personal disciples concerning help when they should be persecuted cannot be legitimately used to comfort a lazy or indifferent modern preacher.

There is one promise, however, that Jesus gave his disciples which experience will justify us in taking as universally applicable. He said in Luke 11:13 that the Heavenly Father would give the Holy Spirit to those who ask. Where Luke quotes Jesus as saying the Holy Spirit, Matthew says (7:11) good things. Jesus encourages us here by telling us that the Heavenly Father is more willing to give the Holy Spirit than an earthly parent is to give good things to his children. Nothing has been more abundantly vindicated in experience than has the statement that God will give his presence and power to those who seek in prayer.

III

The main work of the Holy Spirit in the Synoptics is in relation to Jesus.

The first thing that meets our attention here is that according to Matthew (1:18-21) and Luke (1:26-38), Jesus was begotten in the womb of the virgin Mary by the Holy Spirit. Matthew and Luke differ in their account of the matter. It is clear that Matthew tells the story from the standpoint of Joseph, while Luke tells it from the standpoint of Mary. It is also plain that each account means to say that Jesus was born without a human father. I think it is quite probable that Luke got the story from Mary herself while he was waiting with Paul at Caesarea before sailing for Rome.

Luke 1:35 seems to make the sonship of Jesus to depend on his being thus supernaturally begotten of the Holy Spirit. If Jesus was a son of God only in the general sense in which other men are sons of God, then it would be quite difficult to believe in his virgin birth. But if historic Christianity has been correct in holding that he was the Son of God in a unique and exclusive sense, then it becomes a different matter. The New Testament and historic Christianity have given him an altogether unique place in human life and history. He stands in a class by himself. As a matter of fact, no other approaches him. To believe in an exceptional birth for him is to my mind easier than to believe that he came into the world in the ordinary way. His was no ordinary life. He died no ordinary death. Christianity is founded on the fact of his resurrection. The virgin birth fits in with his sinless life, vicarious death and triumphant resurrection. To believe in the virgin birth of Jesus is, therefore, not to believe in an abnormal prodigy in the biological world, but to believe in the miraculous birth of one who lived on a plane above all other men, who died in a way that had significance for man's relation to God, one who conquered death and lives forevermore above the reach of sin and finite limitations.

Of course, if one is going to proceed on the *apriori* assumption that miracles are impossible, then of course he will not believe in the virgin birth of Jesus. But neither will he believe in the sinless life of Jesus, nor in his unique sonship nor in any miraculous works attributed to him, nor in any saving significance attached to his death, nor in his resurrection. In that case Jesus died and remained dead, and Christianity was one more beautiful dream that turned out to be only an illusion. I am not saying this on the ground that the virgin birth must first be established and everything else made to depend on that. I am saying it on the ground that the virgin birth as presented by Matthew and Luke fits in with the rest of the New Testament picture of Jesus and with the place he has occupied in historic Christianity.

Luke 1:35 says that the Holy Spirit should come upon Mary and that the power of the Highest should overshadow her. As a consequence, that which should be born of her should be holy, the Son of God. The overshadowing power of God explains why Mary was the mother of him who was in a peculiar and exclusive sense the Son of God.

In connection with the account of the baptism of Jesus we are told that the Spirit came upon him (Mark 1:9-11; Matthew 3:13-17; Luke 3: 21-22). Mark and Matthew say that Jesus saw the Spirit descending upon him as a dove. Luke says that the Spirit in bodily form as a dove descended upon him. No explanation is given as to the meaning of the coming of the Spirit upon Jesus. But in John's Gospel (1:31-34) it is indicated that John the Baptist recognized him as the Son of God in that he saw the Spirit descending and abiding upon him.

Following the baptism of Jesus, Matthew indicates that the Spirit led him into the wilderness to be tempted of the devil (4:1). Before entering upon his public ministry he must be tested. The very fact that he was led into the wilderness by the Spirit would imply that there was divine purpose in what followed; but Matthew expressly says that it was for the purpose of his being tempted. Mark says (1:12) that the Spirit "drives" him. There was a strong inner impulsion from God to go into the wilderness, no doubt to contemplate what had taken place and to decide what should be his line of procedure for the future.

Luke's statement implies not only that he was led by the Spirit into the wilderness but also that he was led by the Spirit during the forty days (4:1). Following the account of the temptations, Luke says (4:14) he returned into Galilee in the power of the Spirit. Luke's statements concerning the Spirit's relations to Jesus are quite significant. The Spirit led Jesus into the wilderness and led him during the forty days. Then he returned to Galilee "in the power of the Spirit." The plain implication of these statements is that it was in the power of the Spirit that Jesus met and conquered the devil. It was not in the power of man alone that he conquered the enemy of mankind. It was in the power of God. Other men may feel their independence of God, but when they do they fall. Jesus depended wholly on God's power and conquered. He came back to Galilee, not as a military hero with flying banners and marching armies. In the wilderness, through God's power, he rose above such worldly ideals of success and came back rather a lowly one, but as one who had won victory over the evil one and all his subtle schemes.

We see so far, then, that Jesus was begotten of the Spirit in the womb of the virgin, that he was anointed of the Spirit at his baptism and that in the wilderness he achieved victory in the power of the Spirit. Are we not safe in inferring from these facts that his whole development as a man of complete obedience to God and in a life of righteousness came about by virtue of his being entirely under the control of the Spirit of God? His life is not a demonstration of what man can achieve within himself, not a manifestation of any capacities resident in human nature apart from God, but rather a demonstration of man's spiritual capabilities when completely controlled by God and his Spirit. Nor should we think of the sinless life of Jesus, his victory over sin and the devil, as the result of his having in him some impersonal something that we call a "divine nature" that guaranteed, almost as a mechanical nesessity, his being kept from sin. We should rather think of his holy character and life as being the consequence of his living in complete dependence on the Father and his will. This he was enabled to do by virtue of the indwelling and control of the Spirit. And in this respect he is the Christian's example and ideal. What he did, so can we, at least in measure. As he was indwelt, controlled, led by the Spirit, so should we be.

Not only was he controlled in all his messianic mission and activity, as we shall immediately see, but also his whole inner life was under the control and power of the Spirit. According to Luke's order of events, it was in the hour that he heard the report of the seventy after their return from their triumphant mission (10:21) that Jesus rejoiced in the Holy Spirit and gave thanks to the Father for his manner of concealing things from the wise and prudent and revealing them to babes. When Jesus thus gives thanks to God for disclosing his secrets to the meek and lowly, he is only expressing what he has learned in his own experience with the Father through the Spirit.

The significance of the coming of the Spirit upon him at his baptism may be gathered from a passage like Luke 4:18-19 (cf. Matthew 12:17-21). **When** Jesus goes back to Nazareth, he goes to the synagogue on the sabbath as his custom was. When given an opportunity to read and speak to the people, he reads from Isaiah 61:1, where the Servant says, "The Spirit of the Lord is upon me." Then following the quotation from Isaiah, he goes on to enumerate his messianic works. Evidently, then, the Spirit came upon him to qualify him for his work as God's messianic Servant. He was anointed to preach the gospel to the poor, to proclaim release to the captives, recovering of sight to the blind, to set at liberty those that were bruised, to proclaim the acceptable year of the Lord.

An examination of the items in this program will reveal that it can be summed up in the statement that it was to make men whole. In places where Jesus healed people of sickness or infirmity, the Greek New Testament uses the term "σώζω" (save) to describe what he did. Sometimes the King James Version and the American Standard Version translate this to make whole (Mark 5:34, and others). The work of Jesus was to make people whole. There is a false notion abroad in the world that the coming of the divine into human life perverts the human. Men think that, to be truly human, man must be self-contained and the divine must be shut out. Much of modern thought is founded on this false assumption. Nothing could be further from the truth. This idea is the exact opposite of the truth. One might as well assume that a plant, in order to be normal and healthy must be shut off from air and sunshine. The presence of God is to the human soul what sunshine and air are to the plant. Man perishes without God. And the work of Jesus as set out in our Gospels was to bring God into the lives of men in physical, mental, and spiritual healing power.

To this end he was anointed of the Spirit of God. He was utterly given over to the Spirit. He was completely possessed of the power of God. The Spirit of the Lord was upon him to do the work of God.

Jesus was conscious of a divine mission. He knew that he was sent of God. At the age of twelve there seemed to be a consciousness of a special relation to God and a special mission for God. This came to such fulness at his baptism, or before, that it was the controlling passion of his life. The temptations in the wilderness (and in his life) were the efforts of the devil to sway him from that path or pervert his conception of the end and method of attaining the end. But he was so utterly possessed of God's power and filled with God's Spirit that all these efforts failed.

The other side of this devotion to the will and purpose of God was his devotion to the service of man. He did the will of God in serving man. To cast out evil spirits, to heal men of their physical maladies, to forgive them of their sins, to release them from any and all abnormalities, was to do the will of God. And all this he did in the power of God.

Some men, seeing the works that Jesus was doing, were unable to deny that he was doing these things, but tried to turn men away from him by saying that he was doing these things in the power of the devil (Mark 3: 2-30; Matthew 12:22-37; Luke 11:14-26). It seemed a strange thing to do—to try to discredit one who was doing good by saying that he was doing good in the power of the devil. His good works were so evident that they could not be denied. But these men were not willing to admit that Jesus was God's man doing God's work. That would condemn them. They would have to admit the claims of Jesus as one sent from God. Moreover, it would put them in an intolerable position. It would condemn their teachings and practices. At all costs they would not do that. They must keep up their barriers of defense against Jesus and his works, no matter what else happened. So they resorted to the desperate expedient of saying in substance: "We know that he is doing these things. He is opening blind eyes, unstopping deaf ears, healing sick people, restoring sanity to unbalanced minds, casting out evil spirits. *But* you had better not follow him. Don't listen to his teaching. Don't yield to his claims. He is doing these things, but he is doing them in the power of the devil. He isn't God's man but Satan's."

Jesus warned these men that they were getting on dangerous ground. He told them that they were in danger of committing an unpardonable sin. Why did Jesus say this?

One of two things must have been true. Either they knew that Jesus was doing these things in the power of God and they willfully lied about it, or they were so blinded by prejudice and hatred that they could not see the truth when it was patent before their eyes.. In either case they were in a desperate condition. I am inclined to believe the former situation was the true one; namely, that they knew that they were lying when they said that Jesus was doing these good works in the power of the devil; that they were deliberately calling white black. If that was the case, they were in danger of perverting their own moral natures utterly and irreparably. They were in danger of losing the power of moral discrimination. In that case they would be hopeless. God must lay hold of a man to save him through the truth. If he cannot perceive truth, for him truth has become falsehood or falsehood has become truth, then there is no way that God can lay hold of him. I think I have known people who told lies so consistently and persistently that they lost the power of discriminating the difference between the truth and a lie so that they did not know when they were lying and when they were telling the truth. I suppose in that case we might say that a man could not tell the truth, because for him truth had lost its identity. His moral nature had lost its power to be made whole.

If the second alternative spoken of above was the real one, that is, that they were so blinded by prejudice and hatred that they could not see that Jesus was doing his works in the power of God, then they were just a little farther down the road to moral and spiritual deterioration and ruin than they would have been if the first alternative were true.

This interpretation would not agree with the views of some of our modern theologians with reference to man. Karl Barth would not allow that there is anything in man by nature that can degenerate in coming in contact with Christ and the gospel. He will not allow that there is anything in man's natural constitution with which the gospel can make connection. There is nothing in man worth saving. All that is worth saving must be created by a fiat of the Almighty. There is no connecting point between man's natural constitution and the gospel.

But I do not so read the mind of Jesus. The impression that one gets from reading the Gospels is that Jesus looked on man as of great value in God's sight, as being the object of God's love and care—all men are thus precious to him. To man's intelligence and moral sense the gospel appeals. By responding to the gospel, man may be saved; by rejecting, he may ruin himself. When speaking of a sin that has no forgiveness, Jesus does not mean that there is any sin that God cannot or will not forgive if man repents. But he may easily mean that a man by the wrong reaction to the grace of God revealed in Christ could put himself in a state where it will be a moral impossibility for him to repent.

As we have already seen, John the Baptist seemed to get a glimpse of the fact that Jesus would usher in a spiritual order. He should baptize in the Holy Spirit. In line with this we find at the end of Luke's Gospel (24:49) that the risen Christ made a promise of "power from on high" to his disciples as he commissioned them to preach to all the nations remission of sins in his name. This promise we find fulfilled in Acts. Thus the end of the Gospels and the book of Acts fit into each other in telling about the Spirit as that Spirit was poured out upon his waiting disciples.

At the end of Matthew (28:19) we have the reference to baptizing into the name of the Father, the Son, and the Holy Spirit. This is taken by many modern critics as not coming from Jesus, but as a later insertion. But there is good evidence that the risen Christ did communicate with his disciples. The transformation that came over them so that they became a victorious band of witnesses to him and his saving power bears testimony to that effect. And if he did so communicate with them, there is no reason why he might not have spoken these words as here represented. A brief statement will be made later about the Trinitarian aspect of this matter.

CHAPTER IV

THE HOLY SPIRIT IN THE BOOK OF ACTS

In the first chapter of Acts, we find the Holy Spirit mentioned four times. In verse two, Luke tells us that during the forty days following the resurrection the risen Christ gave commandment to the apostles through the Holy Spirit. In verse sixteen, Peter tells the band of one hundred twenty that it was necessary that the Scripture should be fulfilled which the Holy Spirit spoke by the mouth of David concerning Judas. In verses four and five, the disciples are re minded of a promise from the Father to the effect that they should be baptized in the Holy Spirit not many days hence.

The important passage in the first chapter is verse eight. When the disciples asked Jesus if he would at that time restore the kingdom to Israel, Jesus an swered that it was not for them to know times and seasons which the Father had set within his own authority. But he said: "Ye shall receive power, after that the Holy Ghost [Holy Spirit, ASV] is come upon you: and ye shall be witnesses unto me both in Jerusalem, and in all Judaea, and in Samaria, and unto the uttermost part of the earth." Here we have laid out the program that is followed in the Book of Acts· We have stated what the business of his people is in the world. It is to bear witness to him. It all centers in that. That is the one all-inclusive function of Christians in the world. It is to let the world know by word of mouth and in every way possible what they know about Jesus Christ. They are to tell a story, and that story is about Jesus.

Then their field of operation is marked out. They are to begin where they are, at Jerusalem. Then they are to reach out to Judea and Samaria and to the uttermost part of the earth. They are to begin where they are and go to the last place in the world. They are to leave nobody out. They are to take in the last man in the world. Every man must hear his testimony.

They are also told what their equipment is to be. They should receive power (δύναμις) when the Holy Spirit should come upon them. The Holy Spirit himself was to be that power. It was not power that would in any way inhere in the disciples. It would not in any possessive sense be theirs. When it in any possessive sense became theirs, they would lose it. It was power given, bestowed from God. The power, in fact, would be God himself with, upon, and in them.

This promise in Acts 1:8 is a reaffirmation of a promise given by the risen Christ as recorded in Luke 24:49. Luke tells us then that Jesus had given his disciples a commission to preach repentance and remission of sins in his name to all the nations. But they were first to wait at Jerusalem for the promise of the Father. They were not ready. They should tarry until they were clothed with power from on high. Luke again represents the risen Lord as saying to the apostles in Acts 1:4-5 that they should wait for the promise of the Father, and that not many days hence they should be baptized in the Holy Spirit.

II

These indications that something new was coming were realized on the Day of Pentecost. The account is given in the second chapter of Acts. It is impossible to overemphasize the importance of this event in the founding of the Christian religion and for the religious history of mankind.

Perhaps a word should be said about the Day of Pentecost. Pentecost was a Jewish festival that came fifty days after Passover. Passover is perhaps the best known of all Jewish feasts. It celebrated the deliverance of the people of Israel from Egyptian bondage. The blood of the Passover lamb reminded the Jews of the deliverance of their first-born when the death angel went through the land of Egypt and slew the first-born of every Egyptian household. Paul speaks of Christ as our Passover. Doubtless the apostle means to say that it is through the sacrifice of Christ that we are delivered from a greater bondage —the bondage of sin.

Pentecost came fifty days later and was the feast of harvest. (See Leviticus 23:15ff.) Is it too much, then, to see in the coming of the Holy Spirit on the Day of Pentecost the fulfilment of the promise of harvest in the gospel? The Holy Spirit is the power of God working to bring to realization in human experience the blessings promised in the gospel. Pentecost was the releasing among men of the redemptive power of Christ. It was the realization in the experience of man of that which was made possible in the death and resurrection of Jesus. Pentecost was just as essential for the realization in the lives of men of the values of the gospel as was Calvary and the resurrection. Without the death and resurrection of Jesus there would be no gospel. Without Pentecost there would be no gospel so far as our apprehension and experience are concerned.

Pentecost was, first of all, the release of power for preaching the gospel. Jesus had commissioned his people to preach repentance and remission of sins in his name to all the nations (Luke 24:45-49). He had told them that they should bear witness to him to the last place on earth (Acts 1:8). But he had indicated that they were not ready (Luke 24:49). They should wait. They should tarry at Jerusalem. That is what we find them doing in the first chapter of Acts. After Jesus ascended they waited together for ten days. They prayed (Acts 1:14). We can be quite sure that they were praying about what Jesus had promised, about their enduement with power for the work which he had commissioned them to do.

The first four verses of the second chapter of Acts give a simple, prosaic account of certain things that took place. These facts, however simple they are in their recital, were of tremendous importance in their significance. They bear mainly on one point: the Spirit's work in qualifying those early disciples to bear witness to Jesus. Some of the statements must have been intended to have a symbolical significance: "the sound as of the rushing of a mighty wind"; "it filled all the place where they were"; "tongues parting asunder as of fire"; they "began to speak with other tongues."

This "sound as of the rushing of a mighty wind" must have been a sound similar to that of a tornado. A tornado is practically irresistible in its power. The only safe place when one strikes is in a cave below the surface of the ground. The same word in the Greek Testament is used for wind and spirit. This sound as of the rushing of a mighty wind must have been meant to symbolize the power of the Spirit—the power with which these disciples were to bear witness to Jesus and his saving grace.

The "tongues parting asunder as of fire" evidently also were meant to symbolize the power of the testimony with which these Christians were speaking of the living Christ and his saving power.

"They spoke in other tongues as the Spirit gave them utterance." It would seem from this that these followers of Jesus were given the power to speak in other languages. It is said soon after this that the people, assembled from many countries and provinces, heard them speak each in his own language. This has been disputed, but I hardly see how we can deny that this is what the author of Acts meant to say.[1]

When Peter was called upon to explain what was taking place, it is instructive to note the line that he followed. The bystanders had accused the disciples of being drunk. This indicates that they were acting in such a way as to make the impression that they were under the control of some powerful and unusual influence. Peter explains it by saying that this was the thing that had been set forth through the prophet Joel (2:28ff.). Joel had said that in the last days (the messianic age) God would pour forth of his Spirit upon all flesh and that they should prophesy.

What was taking place he affirms was the fulfilment of this prophecy of Joel. Two points are worthy of notice. One is that what was taking place was the result of the outpouring of God's Spirit. The fact

[1]See Carver, *Commentary on Acts;* Stifler, *Introduction to Acts,* and Dana, *The Holy Spirit in Acts,* and others. *Per contra,* see *Speaking in Tongues,* by D. A. Hayes, and *The Spirit,* by Streeter (editor), chapter V by Anderson-Scott.

that it was the fulfilment of prophecy shows that it was not something new in the sense that it was not anticipated and not prepared for. It was anticipated. We have already seen that in the Gospels and the first chapter of Acts, Jesus as well as John the Baptist had anticipated this thing. Peter's quotation from Joel and his interpretation of the quotation show that it was anticipated even in Old Testament religion. This thing that was taking place, then, was not new in the sense that it was entirely unrelated to the past. The whole historical context in which it takes place shows that it was the outgrowth and development of God's past dealings with Israel.

It was, however, so unusual that the onlookers were astonished. They were taken completely aback at what they were seeing. These disciples were evidently under the control of some unusual power. Peter says that that power was not strong drink but the Spirit of God.

A second thing to notice is that in line with Joel's prophecy, the Spirit was to come on all God's people. The Spirit was to be poured out on old and young, male and female. All God's people were to possess the Spirit and all were to prophesy. That is one difference between the old order and the messianic age.

One of the most important features about Peter's explanation of what was taking place was the way he connected it up with Jesus. The main part of Peter's address had to do with him. He gave a brief recital of the facts relating to him. Peter told about his life, death, and resurrection. But it was the resurrection that he dwelt on. He went back to the sixteenth psalm and interpreted it as being fulfilled in the resurrection of Jesus. He stressed the idea that the psalm did not refer to David. David died, and his tomb was still there as a testimony to the fact that he was still dead. He died and remained dead. David, he said, as a prophet, foresaw the resurrection of Jesus. His resurrection was the fulfilment of the promise made to David that one of his descendents should inherit his throne and reign forever. He refers to another psalm, the one hundred tenth, and interprets it in a messianic sense. He summarizes his discourse concerning Jesus by saying, "Let all the house of Israel therefore know assuredly, that God hath made that same Jesus, whom ye have crucified, both Lord and Christ." It is important to notice, then, that the main significance of what was taking place on the Day of Pentecost was in relation to Jesus Christ. This ought to be seen clearly and be kept in the forefront. The whole meaning of Pentecost is in relation to Jesus Christ. The matter has sometimes been set out in such a way as to make the impression that the Holy Spirit came to take the place of Christ. That impression is carried almost to the point of saying that the Spirit was displacing Christ. That idea is quite erroneous. We repeat that Peter kept Christ at the center. Pentecost was the releasing of the redemptive power of Christ among men. Pentecost was the making of the redemptive power of Christ available for men.

Notice that it was this same Jesus whom they crucified that God had exalted. The fact that it was this same Jesus guarantees the moral and spiritual quality of the power that was working in their midst. Some universal power was working. What was its nature? What was its moral quality? The fact that it was related to this same Jesus makes it possible for them to know its quality. In fact, it makes it impossible for them to mistake its quality. They could know

the quality of this power by looking back to Jesus—
by remembering his words, his deeds of healing, his
life of service. This guaranteed the thoroughly benevolent quality of this power. This assures us that
anything out of harmony with the character of Jesus
Christ is not really done in the power of the Holy
Spirit, no matter what the doer of it may claim. This
makes Jesus Christ—his life, character, and spirit—
the fundamental test that should be applied to any
work wrought as in the power of the Holy Spirit. If
the result does not square with the known character
and work of Jesus Christ, it cannot be recognized as
produced by the Spirit of God. God does not work a
work of one spiritual quality through Jesus and
something of a different quality by the Holy Spirit.

This Jesus had been made both Lord and Christ.
Men had crucified him. They had with wicked hands
put him to death.[2] But in harmony with the fore-
knowledge and determinate counsel of God he had
been raised from the dead and forever put beyond
the power of wicked hands to harm. They might now
lay hold on his followers. They might persecute and
even slay them. In fact, they will thus treat some of
them a little later. But he, the Jesus whom they crucified, is now in his own person beyond their power.
They cannot now touch him with their wicked hands.
More than that, he was enthroned in God's universe.
Men talk about his coming back and being seated on
a material throne in a political or quasi-political
kingdom. What a travesty! He is already seated at
the right hand of God. This is oriental imagery
signifying that under God he has been made Lord of
the universe. While he was here, he was limited,

---

[2]Dr. J. R. Sizoo, in *Interpretation*, April, 1947, *claims* that the Jews did
not kill Jesus. Unfortunately, Peter and the whole New Testament are
against him.

cramped in a life lived in the flesh. In the flesh he was put to death, but raised in the power of the Spirit. Forever he was exalted to the throne in an eternal, spiritual Kingdom. He has now been given the authority and power that rightfully belong to him as Lord and Christ.

Peter connects what was happening at Pentecost directly with the risen Lord. He says that, being seated at the right hand of God and having received from the Father the promised Holy Spirit, Christ poured forth this which they were seeing and hearing. Thus he attributes the coming and working of the Spirit to Christ. He, the living Christ, was doing this work in their midst.

This is in line with the promise that Christ should baptize in the Holy Spirit. It agrees with the manner in which Luke begins this book. He refers to his former book (the Gospel) in which he told of what Jesus began to do and teach. This book is not the Acts of the Apostles. Some of the apostles are barely mentioned in the book. It has been suggested that it is the Acts of the Holy Spirit.[3] That would be nearer its real theme. But perhaps Luke's thought was that he would tell what the ascended, glorified Christ did by his Spirit through his people.

One of my former teachers, Dr. B. H. Carroll, used to remind us that the expression "baptism of the Holy Spirit" did not represent New Testament thought. He said, and rightly so, that in this transaction Christ was the actor or agent, and the Holy Spirit was the medium. Christ baptized his people in (or with) the Spirit.

What we have here in the book of Acts is Christ himself continuing to work in the lives of men. He

[3]See *The Acts of the Holy Spirit*, by A. T. Pierson.

begins now a new phase of his activity. He has lived, died, and risen from the dead. He now sits at the right hand of God. He reigns as King in God's kingdom. He works now in and through the Holy Spirit.

As we go through the New Testament studying this subject, we will see that the Holy Spirit is the Spirit of Christ; that the Holy Spirit is the presence of the living Lord Jesus in spiritual power in the lives of men. This living Lord has not taken his hands off human history. While he was here in the flesh he was only beginning to act and influence men. The hope of human history is that he continues to work. The hope of this world is that Jesus Christ, the reigning Sovereign in God's kingdom, will pour fresh accessions of spiritual power into human history. About the time that the wise of earth decide that the Christian cause is as good as dead, the dead comes to life and moves forward with fresh power. The living Christ acts on human history from above. He works not only horizontally but perpendicularly.

III

One thing that will help us to understand Pentecost is to take a look at the results that came out of this occurrence.

When the people heard what Peter had to say about Jesus, they were "pricked in their hearts." Peter had not minced words in bringing home to them their guilt in crucifying Jesus and his words struck home. Their consciences were aroused, and they came to have a keen sense of their guilt. Then they cried out and said, "What shall we do?"

Two things combined here to bring home to the people their sense of guilt on account of their wicked deeds. One was the plain preaching of Peter telling them of their responsibility in crucifying Jesus, and the other was the power of the Spirit. These two things are always the essential features in bringing home to men a sense of their guilt. Pious platitudes expressed in honeyed words will never bring men to a sense of guilt for sin. On the other hand, the kind of preaching that brings conviction for sin is more than dogmatic denunciation. The conviction of (or for) sin that brings evangelical repentance is more than a feeling of being mean or "bad." It is more than regret that leads to remorse. It brings men to cry, "What shall we do?" with the full intention of doing what the gospel directs that they should do.

This is worth dwelling on. I have seen men in the pulpit denouncing sinners who were already very well aware that they were not what they should be. The preacher would sometimes in an assumed attitude of superiority and bravado "lay it on" to his heart's content. He would denounce men for having fallen short of the spiritual requirements of the divine law or for violating the standards of moral decency. Such preaching may lead to moral reformation, usually temporary in its character and results.

The deficiency in such preaching is that it is not preaching the gospel. The gospel centers in Christ and what he has done for men. Its main theme is not what man has done or failed to do. It is a message about what GOD has done for man in Christ. Such denunciatory preaching as above described centers after all in man, what he has done or failed to do, and what he should do. It really allows for no repentance. There is no place for repentance in such a scheme of things. Man does not repent in view of what he has done or not done, nor in view of what he is called on to achieve. He repents in view of what

God has done for him in Christ Jesus. It is only the
message of the gospel that calls for repentance and
has a place for repentance. Such preaching as we
have been speaking of is easier for the preacher to
do and more flattering to his pride of accomplishment. It is more effective sometimes in producing
temporary results that can be counted, but it is less
effective in bringing permanent, spiritual fruit. It
has been quite prevalent, and still is, in a certain irresponsible and self-inflated type of evangelism.
When Peter called for repentance, he was calling for
a thorough change of mind, a change that really
meant a new spiritual character.[4] The gospel of
Christ is the only message in the world that will
produce such a change.

The other factor that produced this sense of guilt
followed by repentance was the Holy Spirit poured
out on this company of believers by the living Christ.
The Holy Spirit is the Spirit of God as holy working
to produce holiness in man. He works, however, not
in abstracto, but using the gospel message as the
means. By a spiritual religion some modern men
have meant a religion of ethical or esthetic refine-
ment. With some it is little more than a type of refined humanism. The power working on the Day of
Pentecost and causing men to cry out. "What shall
we do?" was more than the power of a refined ethical
or esthetic ideal. It was the power of God energizing
in the hearts and lives of men. It was the power of
God as holy revealing himself in what he had done
and was doing for men in and through Jesus of Nazareth, now being manifested as the Lord of life and
death—the Lord of life who has conquered death and

---

[4] See *The Meaning of Repentance,* chap. IV, by William Douglas Chamber-
lain.

by conquering death manifesting himself as able to conquer sin.

There is no message that man can invent or discover through which the power of God works to transform sinful men into saints. Only the message of the gospel will do this for men, and that message is not man's invention. It is a revelation. It was revealed in history in Jesus Christ. Now it is being revealed in experience through the power of the Holy Spirit.

One noticeable feature of this transaction on the Day of Pentecost was the note of joy that we hear. Luke says that "they took their food with gladness and singleness of heart" (2:46). We hear this kind of a note throughout the book of Acts. From the description given, there was evidently a new type of psychological experience being created in the lives of these believers. The expression that they were filled with the Holy Spirit found in chapter two, verse four, and frequently in this book suggested that this was in reality a new experience. It had to do with the inner life of the people. This inner joy seems to have been of the very nature of the experience. It was not something in addition to the experience but rather an essential feature of it. In some groups today, Acts 2:38 is emphasized as stating the conditions of salvation. Peter told these people, when they inquired what to do, to repent and be baptized into the remission of sins and they should receive the Holy Spirit. He goes on to say that the promise, i.e., the promise of the Holy Spirit as given in the Old Testament,[5] was to them (the Jews)

---

[5]See marginal references in ASV.

and to their children and to those afar off (the Gentiles) and to as many as the Lord should call.

This was not just a matter with them of accepting a creed, submitting to baptism and being enrolled as a member of the church. They heard the word, they believed, they were given a transforming experience, and they were bound together in a fellowship that was stronger than the bonds of family or race.

One of the outstanding features of the account is this fellowship with which they were bound together.[6] The word "church" is not used to describe the company in the early chapters of Acts. Whatever of organization they may have had, the outstanding thing was the fellowship.[7] They attended constantly on the teaching of the apostles and the fellowship, on the breaking of bread (the Lord's Supper?) and the prayers (2:42).

The bond of fellowship was so strong that those who believed were together and had all things common. They (at least many of them) sold their possessions and goods, and distribution was made according as any man had need. This was not even akin to modern communism. It was an entirely voluntary matter, as we see a little later in Acts (chapter five). It does show the strength of Christian love that was active in their midst. It certainly is no model for the organization of modern society. It can be taken as a demonstration of the power of Christian love under the leadership of the Holy Spirit. It is a rebuke to the selfishness of modern, half-hearted Christians who are much more concerned about accumulating

----

[6]See the chapter on Pentecost by Anderson-Scott in *The Spirit,* by Streeter and others.
[7]That is true of the church in the New Testament as a whole.

and holding on to their worldly goods than they are about helping their fellow men or even their fellow Christians in need.

IV

How was the gift of the Spirit in the book of Acts related to baptism? It is evident that there was no essential connection between baptism and the gift of the Spirit. This can be seen by examining three instances. In chapter eight, we have the record of the conversion of the people of the city of Samaria. Philip went to this city and preached and many people were converted and "there was much joy in that city." The group were baptized including Simon Magus. Afterwards Peter and John went down and prayed for them and laid their hands on them and they received the Holy Spirit. In this case clearly baptism preceded the reception of the Spirit. The reception of the Spirit on the part of the converts came sometime after baptism.

We find a similar example in Acts 19. In this case Paul came in contact with a group of believers at Ephesus. When he asked them if they had received the Holy Spirit when they believed, they said that they had not even heard that there was such a thing as the Holy Spirit. They said they had been baptized into John's baptism. Paul instructed them more fully, had them baptized into the name of Jesus, laid his hands on them and the Holy Spirit came on them and they spoke with tongues and prophesied. Here are two instances where people were baptized before they received the Holy Spirit. In each case they received the Holy Spirit when apostles laid their hands on them.

In the tenth chapter of Acts, we have a different order of events. It is the case of Cornelius and his household. Peter preached to them, and while Peter preached to them "the Holy Spirit fell on all them that heard the word." It is after that that Peter inquired about baptizing them in water. In the next chapter (v. 15), Peter refers to it as a baptism in the Spirit. This took place before they were baptized in water. Clearly, then, there was no essential connection between baptism and the gift of the Spirit. This case shows clearly that baptism is not a condition of salvation, because it is said that the Holy Spirit fell on them and they spoke with tongues before anything was said about their being baptized in water. Clearly baptism in the Spirit preceded baptism in water.

In the Epistles of Paul, it is clear that every believer, when he believed, received the Spirit. Thereby he was made a Christian. This constituted him a child of God. But what Paul calls the gifts of the Spirit (*charismata*) seems to be different. Receiving the Spirit was one thing; the *charismata* was another, at least they were distinguishable. They might come together or they might not. Receiving the Spirit was essential to being a Christian. That was a matter of spiritual character. Receiving the gifts of the Spirit (the *charismata*) was not an essential matter, and was not always necessarily a matter of spiritual character. This distinction between the gift of the Spirit and the gifts of the Spirit does not seem to be kept clear in Acts. In Paul's thought, the gift of the Spirit is God's gift to the believer; the gifts of the Spirit (the *charismata*) are gifts bestowed by the Spirit on the believer.

V

We need now perhaps to give a little more particular attention to the work of the Spirit in the expanding missionary work as it is set out in Acts. The work started at Jerusalem. It started as a Jewish movement. But according to the program laid out in Acts 1:8, it was not to be confined to the Jews. The movement was to reach out beyond Jerusalem and Judea. It was to reach to Samaria and to the uttermost part of the earth.

One providential factor that was used to push the disciples out from Jewish boundaries was persecution. These Jewish Christians, it seems, might have been content to hover around the home base in Jerusalem. But persecution arose and scattered them abroad except the apostles who remained at Jerusalem. And as they went, they went preaching.

Philip went to Samaria; and, as we have seen, many turned to the Lord; and Peter and John went to Samaria and laid their hands on the converts and they received the Holy Spirit. Perhaps one purpose in the coming of the Spirit on those disciples was that it might be made clear that it was the will of the Lord that the Samaritans should receive the gospel.

A little later the Spirit helped to prepare Peter for preaching to Cornelius and his company (10:19). The Lord worked both with Cornelius and with Peter. Peter was finally brought to Caesarea and preached to Cornelius and the company gathered at his house. They were converted and again the Holy Spirit fell on them. Again it was made clear that it was God's will that the gospel should reach out beyond the borders of Judea, that it should go to the Gentiles.

A little later the apostles and the whole company of Christians faced the question as to whether the gospel should be preached to the Gentiles—whether this movement should remain a Jewish movement or should become more than that. Certain men went down to Antioch, to which Paul and Barnabas had returned from their triumphant missionary journey. These men contended that for Gentiles to become Christians they must be circumcised and keep the Jewish law. Without this, the Judaizers contended, Gentiles could not be saved. They had a head-on collision with Paul. He contended that faith in Jesus was sufficient for the salvation of anyone, Jew or Gentile. It was decided that there should be a conference on this matter at Jerusalem. We are not concerned here with the details of that conference. We are concerned with the fact that the Holy Spirit guided the conference in its decisions.

At the beginning of the conference, Peter recited how God had used him to preach to the Gentiles and how God had given the Holy Spirit to the Gentiles who believed even as he had given to believing Jews.

The decisions of the conference were issued in a statement beginning "it seemed good to the Holy Spirit and to us." The Gentile converts were advised to "abstain from things sacrificed to idols, and from blood, and from things strangled, and from fornication." From our point of view today, there might be some question about putting some of these things touching matters of Jewish law in the same category with a moral question like fornication. But the main question we are concerned with is that the Holy Spirit led these early Christians to break away from narrow Jewish limitations and reach out into the Gentile world to carry the gospel.

We have seen how Jewish limitations were broken through in the case of Philip's preaching at Samaria and in the preaching of Peter to Cornelius and his company at Caesarea, and how in each of these cases the Holy Spirit came upon the believers, thus sealing with divine approval the work of extending the gospel beyond narrow Jewish limitations. It was quite difficult for some of these early Jewish Christians, even among the apostles, to break away from their Jewish training and prejudices and associate with Gentiles in the gospel. That is plainly evident in the case of Peter as his experience is recorded in Acts, chapter ten.

The final and decisive step in breaking over racial lines and religious prejudices to set the gospel free as a universal gospel available to all men on conditions that are universal in their nature came with the work of Paul. It is not necessary to go here into an account of the training and conversion of Saul of Tarsus. It might be well to point out two or three things. One is that when the Lord needed a man to set out the gospel as universal in nature, available to all men on conditions that were essentially universal, first of all, he chose a Jew. Looking back on the matter from our vantage point, we can see that it would have been difficult for a Gentile of that day to have had the background necessary for such a work. Some moderns who think that Paul's gospel was a composite of diverse elements including some from Judaism and some from the mystery religions of his day and some from perhaps other sources, would not agree with my position. I have no hope of agreeing with them, nor do I have any hope that such thinkers would agree with me. Paul's theology was no such eclectic, intellectual system.   Paul's message was a gospel, not an intellectual philosophy of life in general. And Paul's gospel involved certain fundamental principles of Old Testament religion that it would have been difficult for a Gentile to grasp and hold as Paul did.   The gospel of Christ has roots back in Old Testament religion; and if that gospel were uprooted from its Old Testament background, it would be a marvel if it did not become something other than the gospel of Christ.   This does not mean that the gospel cannot be transplanted to Gentile soil.   Paul insisted that it could and should. But at the same time he insisted that it should remain the gospel.   That is where the danger would have come if the gospel had not been transplanted by a Jew.   For instance, there would have been danger that the gospel would lose its doctrine of one God, holy and righteous in character, distinct from the world of nature and mankind, if its fundamental formulation for the Gentile world had been made by a non-Jewish mind.   Likewise, one can see how the doctrine of faith might have lost its real meaning under different circumstances.   The Old Testament doctrine of sacrifice was quite a help, if not essential, in interpreting the meaning of the cross.

It would have been difficult for a doctrine of the Holy Spirit to come out of the Gentile world of Paul's day.   That world knew spirits in abundance, but not one of these spirits was *holy* in the biblical sense of that term.   The Spirit of God in the New Testament is holy as God is holy in Old Testament religion.   He is holy as Jesus Christ was holy.   He works to produce holiness in us after the pattern found in our Lord Jesus Christ.   It would have been difficult for one coming out of the Gentile world of that day to conceive and set out a doctrine of Holy Spirit such as we find in Paul. I think, then, that we are safe in holding that there was divine providence in raising up a missionary to carry this gospel to the Gentile world whose religious conceptions were rooted back in Old Testament religion.

Was there not divine wisdom also in raising up a man to be missionary to the Gentiles who was born and brought up in the Dispersion of that day? Saul of Tarsus was a Jew, but he was a Jew of the Dispersion. He knew the Gentile world of that day at firsthand. He knew its culture, its commerce, something of its political life. He knew also its sins, its failures, and its religious life. He knew its longings and its aspirations. All this qualified him to preach to the people of the Gentile world of his day. In his missionary activity he always went to the synagogue first with his message about Jesus as the Messiah. But when turned out of the synagogue, as he usually was, he knew how to make other contacts and find other places to preach the gospel.

In the eleventh chapter of Acts we have a reference to the scattering of the disciples from Jerusalem because of the persecution that arose about Stephen. Everywhere they went they preached Jesus. Some of them found themselves in Antioch, and they preached to the Greeks as well as to Jews. Many were converted, and there was soon a growing work there. The hand of the Lord was with them. When word of this movement came to the church at Jerusalem, they sent Barnabas to see about the matter. Doubtless the conservative "regulars" at Jerusalem were aroused by the report of Greeks being taken into the movement.

Barnabas was a good man and full of the Holy Spirit and of faith.

Barnabas rejoiced at the good work that was going on, but he soon saw that it was too big for him. He showed himself a man of wisdom. When he had a situation too big for him to handle, he looked for a man who was big enough. He remembered Saul of Tarsus and went and brought Saul to work with him. For a whole year they taught the disciples at Antioch.

Later there was a group of men in the church at Antioch whom Luke describes as prophets and teachers (Acts 13:1). As they ministered to the Lord and fasted, the Holy Spirit said to them that they should separate two of their number to the work to which he (the Spirit) had called them. The two men were Barnabas and Saul. Then after fasting and praying, they sent them forth. Then, Luke says, being sent forth by the Holy Spirit, they went out. Then follows an account of the first great missionary journey of Saul whose name was changed to Paul on this journey.

This was the beginning of Paul's great missionary activity among the Gentiles. On Paul's second missionary journey, we read that he was forbidden of the Holy Spirit to speak the word in Asia (Acts 16:6). Immediately after that he "assayed to go into Bithynia, but the Spirit of Jesus suffered them not" (Acts 16:7). Soon after, Paul and his company were directed by a vision to go over into Macedonia, and he crossed into Europe and preached at Philippi and planted the gospel on the continent of Europe. Wherever Paul went in the work of the Lord, he went bound in the Spirit.[8] Certain

---

[8]See Revised Standard Version on Acts 20:22.

prophets and prophetesses, speaking in the Spirit (21:4, 10-13), tried to keep Paul from making his last journey to Jerusalem. Paul knew also from the Spirit's testimony that bonds and afflictions awaited him but he had gone through all that in his own mind and was ready if need be to die for the Lord in Jerusalem (21:13). We find from 20:28 that Paul believed, not only that the Spirit thrusts out missionaries into new territory but also that the Spirit appointed bishops over established churches.

We see, then, that the Holy Spirit selected certain men for a missionary forward movement. The Spirit directed them in rather minute fashion as to where they should preach. They were forbidden to preach in certain provinces and providentially directed to preach in others. They were led to cross into Europe and start the gospel on its westward course rather than back eastward into Asia.

We thus see that the Spirit calls men to particular work, directs as to where they shall go, and the type of work that they shall do. Especially is it noteworthy that the divine Spirit thrusts men out into the waiting harvest fields of the world of humanity. From that day to this the Spirit of God has been thrusting men out to preach the gospel, trying to get them to carry out the Lord's command to preach the gospel to every man on earth.

One outstanding feature of the work of the Spirit in the book of Acts is that the Spirit is the impulsive power leading men to preach the gospel to others, and the Spirit gives them fruitage in preaching. The Holy Spirit in Acts is the Spirit of evangelism and missions.

Chapter V

JOHN'S DOCTRINE OF THE SPIRIT

As we have seen, there is rather extensive preparation in the Old Testament for the doctrine of the Spirit as given in the New Testament. Of course, in both Old and New Testaments the fundamental conception with reference to God is his unity. In the statement, "Hear, O Israel, the Lord our God is one Lord" (Deuteronomy 6:4), we have the foundation of both Old and New Testament religion. When asked about the first commandment, Jesus quotes this statement, and then, following Deuteronomy, makes it the basis of the commandment to love God with all the heart, soul, mind, and strength (Mark 12:28ff.). Both Deuteronomy and Jesus ground the obligation to love God with all one's being in the fact that God is one. The unity of God calls for the unity of the worshiper. God is one in the sense that he is undivided and in the sense that he is supreme. He could not be supreme if he were divided. And man could not worship with an undivided heart if he worshiped more than one God. The psychologists tell us these days that we need to integrate our personalities. But to worship the one supreme God revealed through Jesus Christ is the only way to bring man to a saving unity within himself over against the distracting world in which he lives.

However, then, we may interpret the Christian doctrine of the Trinity, it must not be so interpreted as to give us three gods nor a divided God.

The God and Father of our Lord Jesus Christ is the sole God of the universe. But, as revealed to us in our Lord Jesus Christ, he is more than the ground and unity of all things sought after by the philosopher; he is a living Personality, a God of love and grace with whom we can have fellowship in worship and prayer, and in the execution of whose purposes we may have a part through a life of service.

I

And the reason we can apprehend this supreme God of the universe as a living, loving personality is because he is revealed to us in a Son who is our sole Lord and Master. Jesus Christ is sole Lord in the same sense that God is sole God. Paul says in 1 Corinthians 12:4-5 that the same God works diversities of gifts. He also says there are diversities of ministrations but the same Lord; and diversities of gifts but the same Spirit. Here we have one God, one Lord Jesus Christ, and one Holy Spirit. If Jesus Christ were not Lord and Saviour in the same absolute and exclusive sense that the Father is God, then he could not reveal God as the supreme and only God in the world.

Nobody presents this in the New Testament more clearly than does John. John regards Jesus as the *only* Son of God. He is not in a class with others in his relation to God. In John's Gospel, Jesus speaks of God as *the* Father and himself as *the* Son in a way that shows he is thinking of his relation to God as Father as unique. Notice how he relates himself to God in chapter five. When the "Jews" attack him for violating their law by curing a man on the sabbath, Jesus answers by saying: "My Father worketh hitherto, and I work." Then they

had other grounds on which to attack him. Now
they said he not only breaks the sabbath but blas-
phemes by calling God his own Father, thus making himself equal with God. If Jesus had not
meant to claim to be the Son of God in an exclusive
sense, in a sense that somehow made him equal
with God, he could very easily have assuaged their
anger by saying something like this: "You mis-
understand me. I do not mean to claim to be the
Son of God in any such sense as that. Please calm
yourselves and let me explain that I only meant
that I am a son of God in the sense that other sons
of Abraham are sons of God." But Jesus did no
such thing. He did just the opposite. He went on
to justify the claim that he was God's only and
unique Son. He claims that he was doing the work
of God. He was doing nothing from himself. He
was doing only what he had seen the Father
doing. He said that because the Father loved (φιλει)
him, he would show him greater works at which
they would marvel. It might be worth noticing that
Jesus uses a word here for the Father's love to him
that is nowhere used in the New Testament for
God's love to unredeemed men, men outside of
Christ. It is a word that denotes personal affection.
It is never used for God's love for man except once
or twice in John's Gospel for God's love for the
personal disciples of Jesus. God's love for us can
become personal affection only as we are made sons
of God by faith in Jesus Christ. But in the case
of Jesus, the Father's love goes out to him as the
Son of God, Son in his own right. Between him
and the Father there was that full and unrestrained
personal affection that is the natural relation of a
Father to an only Son. God's love to mankind as a

whole is the love of rational good will; it can be that of personal affection only as we become identified with the only Son.

Jesus goes on in this passage to claim that the Father has committed to him the power to judge and to give life. These are powers that belong to God, but he has given the right to exercise these functions to the Son. Jesus claimed that even then he had the power to raise men from spiritual death and that in the future he would raise all the dead, some to a resurrection of life, others to a resurrection of condemnation.

The most astonishing thing that Jesus says in this connection is that the Father gives him the power to execute judgment in order that all might honor the Son even as they honor the Father. This is indeed astonishing unless Jesus is the Son of God in an exclusive sense. An early Roman writer described Christians as those who sang hymns to Christ as to God. Historic Christianity has always given to Jesus Christ a place that makes Christians idolaters unless Jesus Christ is truly the sole Son of God.

And what I am saying here is that he could reveal God as the one supreme God because he was the one and only Son of God. No other can be put in a class with him in relation to God or man.

While John sets out that Jesus is the sole Son of God, we should not think that John is here breaking with the Synoptics. He is only bringing out more distinctly what is implicit in the Synoptics. In fact, in places it is rather explicit in these earlier Gospels. There is a passage in Matthew and Luke that has been described as quite Johannine in its character. It is found in Matthew 11:25ff. with the parallel in Luke 10:21ff. Since it is found in Matthew and Luke and not in Mark, it is possible (and I think probable) that it came from Q and therefore should have good critical standing. Anyway, it is to be noticed here that only the Son knows the Father, and still more suprising that only the Father knows the Son. It is worthy of note that Jesus here speaks of God as the Father and himself as the Son in very much of a Johannine tone; and that he seems to be saying that there is a depth of being in himself as the Son that nobody has penetrated except the Father.

In addition to this, it is to be noted that he claims that no one can know the Father except the one to whom he chooses to reveal him as Father. And this is the point that I have been making so far in this chapter; namely, that Jesus as the one and only Son of God and Lord of men could reveal the Father as the supreme and only God of the universe. It is only as men grasp firmly the fact of the sole Lordship of Jesus Chirst that they hold to the idea that the Father is the sole God of the universe in a living way. Otherwise the tendency is to lose God in the powers of nature or the abstractions of man's own mind. Monotheism as a living conviction in the lives of men is wrapped up with faith in Jesus Chirst as the only begotten Son of God and absolute Lord of men's lives. The lives of men can be unified in God only as these lives come under the living control of Jesus Christ as Lord and Master.

II

Now I wish to join up with this another fact, namely, that in the New Testament Christ is recognized as Saviour and Lord in any practical and

living way only in and through the work of the
Spirit of God. Before coming to John on this point,
let us take a look at one or two other portions of
the New Testament. In the sixteenth chapter of
Matthew,[1] when Peter confesses Jesus as the Christ,
the Son of the living God, Jesus pronounces him
blessed and says that flesh and blood had not revealed this fact to him but the Father in heaven.
This was not something that Peter had discovered
for himself but something that had come as a revelation from God. The Holy Spirit is not mentioned
by name here, but it is easy enough to see that this
is in line with the work of enlightenment attributed
to the Spirit in other places. God by his Spirit had
been dealing with Peter.

In the nineteenth chapter of Acts, Paul found
some people at Ephesus who had been baptized, according to their statement, into John's baptism,
but they knew nothing about the Holy Spirit. Paul
gave them further instruction about the relation of
John's work and preaching to Jesus, had them
baptized, laid his hands on them, and the Holy Spirit
came on them. From the fact that Paul spoke to
them about the relation of John's work to Jesus and
from what Paul says elsewhere, my belief is that
Paul had them baptized on the ground that a man
who does not know the Holy Spirit does not in any
vital way know Jesus as Lord and Saviour. Luke
tells us that these people, after Paul's instruction
to them, were baptized into the name of the Lord
Jesus. In 1 Corinthians 12:3, Paul says that no man
can call Jesus Lord save in the Holy Spirit.

Nobody in the New Testament grasps more firmly
than does John the principle that it is only in and

---

[1] Cf. chapter on Synoptics.

through the divine Spirit that we know Christ and his saving work. In fact, the central principle of John's doctrine of the Spirit is to be found right in here. More clearly perhaps than any other New Testament writer, John sets out that the one function of the Holy Spirit is to enable men rightly to relate themselves to Christ. In this respect the Spirit is related to Christ somewhat as Christ is related to the Father. Christ is sent by the Father, is dependent on the Father, and comes to reveal the Father. So the Spirit is sent by Christ, is dependent on him, and has as his one task to reveal Christ to men.

This comes out in the name given to the Spirit when he is called the Spirit of truth. Three times in the Farewell Discourse he is called by this name (14:17; 15:26; 16:13). What does this name suggest to us? Remember that Jesus calls himself the truth (14:6). All the way through this Gospel Jesus is presented as the truth or reality of God in human life. He came to make God known; but he makes God known not just by telling men about God. The prophets of the Old Testament had done that. Words alone are not an adequate revelation of God. Jesus makes God known by being the incarnation, the embodiment of the very life of God. He is the reality of God as objectified and made known in a human life. He is the historical, objective revelation of God.

But an objective, historical revelation of God is not enough. Somehow God must be made living and real to men in their own experiences. To make God thus real and living to men in their own experiences is the work of the divine Spirit. This will help us to understand that verse in John's First Epistle where he says that the Spirit is the truth (1 John 5:7). Christ is the reality of God as revealed objectively in a human life; the Spirit is the reality of God as given in Christian experience. In 1 John, chapter five, the author is telling us that Jesus as the Christ came by water and by blood. An incipient Gnosticism around Ephesus was saying that Jesus was not the Christ, that Jesus was only a mortal man. The Christ, so they said, as some kind of Spirit, came on Jesus at his baptism and left him before he died. So he died not as the Christ, but only as a man. John is insisting over against this that Jesus came as the Christ, not only by the water of baptism but also by the blood of the cross. Not by water only, he says, but by water and the blood is he the Christ.

He also says that there are three that bear witness: the Spirit, the water, and the blood. He further says that these three agree in one. He does not say what the one is in which they agree, but I think the context makes it clear that he means the one point (or idea) that Jesus is the Son of God and that as Son of God he came through the blood of the cross. When he says that there are three that bear witness, I get the impression that he is putting the emphasis on the Spirit. That seems to be implied in the fact that he says that the Spirit is the truth. The Spirit is the truth or reality of God as known through Jesus as the crucified Son of God.

III

In the Gospel of John, the work of the Spirit is definitely made to depend on the work of Christ. In 16:7, Jesus says to his disciples, who seem to be confused because he has told them that he was going away, that it is better for them that he should go. The reason is that, if he does not go, the Comforter or Paraclete will not come to them. But he goes on to say: "If I go away, I will send him unto you." The coming of the Spirit depended on the going of Jesus. The Spirit could not come until Jesus went by way of the cross. Pentecost must follow Calvary and the resurrection. It could not have been the other way. Men could not be clothed with power to preach the gospel until there was a gospel to preach. And in these days it cannot be too strongly emphasized that the gospel centers in a deed of redemption accomplished by Jesus Christ. The gospel is not just some bright and optimistic idea that a preacher thinks up during the week to present to his congregation on Sunday morning. Nor is it a set of abstract and idealistic principles that some philosopher has worked out. Some men wearing the name of Christ tell us today that it would make no difference in their religion if such a man as Jesus had never lived in the world. So far as their religion is concerned, that may be true, but so far as the gospel of Christ is concerned, it does make a difference.

The gospel of Christ is grounded in facts. These facts were the death, burial, and resurrection of Jesus. It is not just bare facts, I admit. It is these facts in relation to our sins. Christ died, but he died for our sins. He rose from the dead according to the Scriptures. The gospel is not a break with the Old Testament. It is the completion of the Old Testament. It is that without which the Old Testament has no meaning, without which the Old Testament comes to naught.

An instructive passage showing the relation of the Spirit to Jesus and his work is 7:37-39. On the last day, the great day of the feast (Tabernacles), Jesus said: "If any man thirst, let him come unto me, and drink." There he indicates that from within the one that believed on him should flow rivers of living water. John then explains the language of Jesus for us by saying that it referred to the Holy Spirit. He then makes what sounds like a strange statement. He says that the Holy Spirit was not yet, because Jesus was not yet glorified. So far as believers were concerned, then, there could be no Holy Spirit in the full Christian sense until Jesus was glorified in death and resurrection. The work of Jesus is first, and the work of the Holy Spirit is to make effective in us what Christ has done for us. Pentecost was the releasing in the world of the redemptive power of Jesus in his death and resurrection.

Another instructive passage on this point is 16:8-15. Jesus says that he will send the Paraclete to his followers; and when he is come, he will convict the world in regard to sin, in regard to righteousness, and in regard to judgment. These are not three separate works of conviction, but one—three phases of one work; and all of it centers in Christ. Men are to be convicted of sin because they believe not on him. They reject him who is the light of the world, and that is the essence of sin. They are convicted of righteousness because he goes to the Father and men see him no more. Perhaps that means something like this. While he was here visible among men, he was a standard of righteousness that men could see. Now that he is going into the invisible world, he would still be such a standard;

but since men could no longer see him, they would need some power to make him real to them. This the Holy Spirit would do. Thereby they would be made conscious of a righteousness which they did not have but which was available in him. They would also be made conscious of a condemnation resting on the world since the world, following the lead of its prince, had rejected Jesus. In condemning Jesus the world had thereby condemned itself

So we see that the convicting work of the Spirit centers entirely in Christ and his work.

After speaking thus about the convicting work of the Spirit, Jesus goes on to tell them that he has many things to say to them, but they cannot (are not able to) bear them now. But he says: "When he, the Spirit of truth, is come, he will guide you into all the truth." Notice that he does not say all truth, as the King James version says; it is all *the* truth. He is not speaking of truth in general, not scientific or philosophical truth; it is gospel truth, truth as revealed in Jesus Christ—truth which Christ himself is. Jesus goes on to say that the Spirit will not speak from himself; but what he should hear that he should speak. Then he says: "He shall glorify me." What does he mean by all this? It sounds like rather strange language. Here is something of what he means. The Spirit is not an agent acting independently of Christ in bringing us into a knowledge of the truth. He does not act apart from Christ; he acts jointly with Christ. He is dependent on Christ. He reveals Christ. Christ is the truth that he enables us to apprehend. The Spirit is like light. Light does not exist so much for its own sake, but rather that we may see other things through the medium of light. The Holy

Spirit is not in the world to call attention of men to himself but rather to bear witness to Christ.

I have read after and heard men talk when they seemed to be saying in substance that the Holy Spirit was an agent acting apart from Christ and independently of him. They seemed to say that we should look to Christ for salvation or justification, and then we should look to the Holy Spirit for assurance or sanctification or power. This is a false impression. Christ is the sole object of faith in the New Testament, and the Spirit is the sole power to enable us to trust him. We should trust him for justification, but also for sanctification, assurance, power, and all else that we need in the Christian life. And the Holy Spirit works all this in us by helping us to trust Christ and rightly relate ourselves to him.[2] This is true everywhere in the New Testament. In John's writings, however, the emphasis is on the union of the believer with Christ. We are in him and he is in us. But there is always back of such language the assumption that it is in and through the Spirit that Christ dwells in us.

Coming back to the language of Jesus in John 16: 8-15, we find that after identifying the work of the Spirit with him and his work, he goes on to identify himself and his work with the Father. All things that are his are the Father's, and the Spirit is to declare these things to the followers of Jesus. Here we have a trinity but it is not a trinity of metaphysical speculation, but of living religious experience.

IV

Our thesis in this chapter is that the Holy Spirit has one mission, and one mission only according

---

[2]For a further development of this thought, see the chapter on Paul.

to John, namely, to bear witness to Christ and to make Christ real to men. This is suggested by Jesus in 14:16, where he says that he will pray the Father and he will send another Comforter or Paraclete. The word that is used here for "another" is a word that means another of the same kind or class. Jesus has been their teacher, guide, friend. Now, since he is going away, the Father will send Another to be their teacher, guide and friend. Jesus speaks here of the Spirit in warm, personal terms, not as if speaking of some impersonal principle or power. He speaks of the Spirit as *he,* or, more specifically, *that One.* John often uses the pronoun *that one* when he wishes to speak of Jesus in an emphatic way. Where he calls the Spirit the Paraclete, or *that One,* he speaks of him in personal terms and also suggests that he is to be to the disciples what Jesus himself has been. Now Jesus is going away, but he assures them that he will not leave them as orphans in the world. Another will come to take his place.

In one place Jesus says that he will send the Spirit from the Father (15:26); in other places he says the Father will send the Spirit in his name or at his request (14:16, 26). For the Spirit to be sent in the name of Jesus means that he is sent as the representative of Jesus, as one who is to carry on his work. In this connection Jesus talks about our praying in his name. This passage is often grossly misunderstood and greatly abused. It means much more than to attach the name of Jesus to our prayers as if it were some kind of a magical formula. Nor does it mean, as so often said, that we are to pray on the basis of the merit of Jesus rather than our own. It means to pray as those who represent

Jesus, as those who are committed to him and his cause, as those whose aim and mission in life are to do his will. The Holy Spirit is the One who is to carry on his work in the world.

In speaking about the Spirit, Jesus says, "I come to you" (14:28). Sometimes Christians speak as if they really were orphans in the world. They lament the absence of Christ. Of course he is not present in physical presence, but he tells us that we have something better than that (16:7). He is present in the Spirit. The presence of the Spirit is the presence of Christ himself. We have in his spiritual presence something better than the disciples had when he was with them in the flesh. We have a Voice more effective in making known the will of God than was the voice that spoke to them in his parables or in the Sermon on the Mount. The Voice that we have is one that is inseparable from spiritual character, and an inner light that is light indeed. How clear that Voice is to us, how distinct is its light in our souls depends on how completely we are given over to the will and way of Jesus our Lord and Saviour. John the Baptist tells us that Jesus should baptize in the Spirit (1:33). After the resurrection he breathed on the disciples and said, "Receive ye the Holy Spirit" (20:22). Pentecost was his gift to the infant church. And I do not believe that Pentecost was meant to be the big end of the Christian movement; it was only the beginning. The One who said, "I have overcome the world," will pour fresh accessions of spiritual power into the hearts of his people when they are ready to receive. But they must also be ready to go out in his name and do his will, to serve him with the power that he gives.

Chapter VI

THE TEACHING OF PAUL:
The Holy Spirit and Salvation

The teaching of the apostle Paul on the subject of the Spirit is the richest section of the biblical material on this subject. It might not be true to say that Paul goes any deeper into this subject than do the Johannine writings (the Gospel and First Epistle), but it certainly is true that Paul goes into the question more extensively and sets out the subject in a more comprehensive and ample manner. No writer in the New Testament sets out the function of the Spirit in the Christian life in such an illuminating and stimulating way as does the great apostle to the Gentiles. Paul more definitely than any other New Testament writer discusses the work of the Spirit as something to be experienced on the part of the recipient.

I

Paul makes the possession of the Spirit to be the essential mark of a Christian. He says in Romans 8:9 that if a man does not have the Spirit of Christ, he is none of his. On the other hand, he says that as many as are led by the Spirit of God, they are the sons of God. The possession of the Spirit, then, is the characteristic mark of a Christian. The thing that constitutes a man a Christian is not primarily a matter of race or nationality or creed but a matter of spirit.

I said just now that it was a matter of possession of the Spirit, meaning that one possesses the Spirit. Paul speaks of it as a man having the Spirit. In this way of putting it, "of the Spirit" would be an objective genitive. But it might be better to speak of the possession of the Spirit in the sense that the Spirit possesses the Christian. This would be more in line with what Paul says when he says that those who are led by the Spirit of God are the sons of God. The Spirit needs to possess us. We cannot possess the Spirit in the sense of controlling the Spirit. The Spirit should direct us, not that we should direct the Spirit. The mark of a Christian is that the Spirit of God controls and directs one's life.

A genuine Christian is one whose life is mastered by the Spirit of God. That is a mark that is not likely to be misinterpreted in its significance.

In Galatians 3:2, Paul says, "Received ye the Spirit by works of law, or by the hearing of faith?" He does not say by *the* works of *the* law, but by works of law. His point is that they did not become Christians by obeying legalistic prescriptions of any kind but by a message that they received by faith. Some have said that Paul is talking about receiving the Spirit in an act of faith distinct from the act of faith in which they received Christ as Saviour. I think this interpretation is wrong. Paul does not mean a reception of the Spirit apart from receiving Christ or subsequent to receiving him. He is talking about the faith in which we receive Christ. Christ is always the object of faith in the New Testament (or God made known in Christ), and the Holy Spirit is the power in which we receive Christ. There is no receiving of the Spirit apart from receiving Christ. On the other hand, receiving Christ is receiving the Spirit. When one receives Christ, he imparts his Spirit to such a person.

In Ephesians 1:13-14, Paul connects three things. These three things are: hearing the word of the gospel, believing it, and being sealed with the Holy Spirit of promise. (Cf. Ephesians 4:30 and 2 Corinthians 1:21-22.) My understanding of the meaning of this sealing is that it is the Holy Spirit placed in the heart of every believer, and that it takes place when one believes. The meaning of this for the believer will be discussed a little later. The point we are interested in here is the fact that God puts his Spirit in the heart of each believer and that this indwelling Spirit marks the believer as a child of God.

II

Paul teaches that the indwelling Spirit bears witness that one is a son of God. He says that the Spirit himself bears witness with our spirit that we are the children of God (Romans 8:16). The indwelling Spirit thus becomes our assurance with reference to our sonship to God. We see, then, two things about our being the children of God. One is that God makes us his children by putting his Spirit in our hearts. The other is that the Spirit creates in us the consciousness that we are the children of God. This is what Paul calls the spirit of adoption or sonship. The Spirit in our hearts causes us to cry "Father" as we look to God (Romans 8:15-16). In Galatians 4:5-6, Paul says that we receive the adoption of sons, and because we are sons, God sent forth the Spirit into our hearts, enabling us to cry "Abba, Father." We receive this adoption of sons, that is, an adoption that makes us sons, by faith in Christ. In the same transaction we receive the Spirit that constitutes us sons, and this Spirit in our hearts creates in us the consciousness of sonship.

Some things about this passage and its content are worthy of consideration. This passage does not mean that the Spirit bears witness *to* our spirits, as if the Spirit were over against our spirit speaking to our spirit in an external or objective fashion. It is not the Spirit of God speaking with my spirit as one man speaks with another. The word for *with* in this connection means conjointly with, together with. It is the Spirit of God conjointly with my spirit that bears testimony that I am a child of God. It is not the divine Spirit saying to me that I am a child of God; it is rather the divine Spirit saying along with my spirit that I am a child of God. It is the indwelling and creative Spirit enabling me to realize for myself that I have this relationship with God.

Paul is evidently using the term spirit (of man) here in the sense of the conscious self. He is saying that man is enabled by the Spirit of God to apprehend for himself the son-Father relationship. Since the days of Immanuel Kant, philosophy has seen and taught that the mind of man in knowing is not a passive instrument simply receiving impressions from without. Knowledge is never communicated to a passive mind. The mind is active and acquires knowledge for itself. Any man who is to any extent an educated man is a self-educated man. Books, teachers, schools only help a man to acquire knowledge for himself. What Paul says here is in line with that principle. The Spirit of God indwelling, interpenetrating man's mind, all man's powers, brings man to the consciousness that he is a son of God.

This consciousness of sonship, however, is not a subjective consciousness without objective ground. It is a consciousness that lays hold of the Word of the gospel. It apprehends the Christ who is presented in the gospel. In the next verse (Romans 8:17), Paul says that we realize that if we are sons then we are heirs, heirs of God and joint-heirs with Christ. It is a consciousness in which we realize that our true relationship to God is in Christ, not in ourselves apart from him. But in Christ we realize that all the riches of God's mercy are ours in Christ. In Christ, we are encouraged to lay hold of these riches, and it is in the Spirit that we are enabled to appropriate these riches.

Paul indicates in the preceding verse (Romans 8:15) something of the character of this consciousness of sonship. It is not a spirit of fear, a spirit of bondage in fear, but a spirit of freedom in which we can look up into the face of God and call him Father.

III

Paul teaches that the Spirit dwelling in our hearts is not only the assurance of present sonship to God, but is also the ground of our assurance of final deliverance from corruption and bondage. This is the meaning of Ephesians 1:13-14 and 4:30. In the latter passage, he says that we are sealed unto the day of redemption. The idea seems to be that the Holy Spirit in us is God's seal pledging him that we shall be finally and completely delivered from sin and corruption. What he means by the day of redemption we see in Romans 8:23. He has just spoken in verse

22 of the whole creation as groaning and travailing in pain together. Then he says (v. 23) that we ourselves groan within ourselves, waiting for the adoption, the redemption of our bodies. The Holy Spirit in us is the assurance that the final and complete deliverance for which we long will one day be ours. Our redemption is not yet completed but it is assured. It is in this sense that Paul says that we are saved in hope. We are looking for something more than we have yet received. We have received enough to long for more. We look forward with eager anticipation. We hope. But ours is not a groundless hope; it has a firm foundation in what God has already done for us.

Dr. A. J. Gordon maintains that this sealing of the Spirit is something God does subsequent, logically and chronologically, to regeneration. It is a stamp of ownership that God puts upon believers who consecrate themselves fully to God. This, he says, "is not conversion, but something done upon a converted soul, a kind of crown of consecration put upon his faith."[1] This, I think, is a misunderstanding. I believe that by the sealing of the Spirit, Paul means the impartation of the Spirit himself to the believer when he believes. This I infer not only from what he says in Ephesians 4:30; 1: 13-14; 2 Corinthians 1:21-22, where he uses the term sealing and related terms, but from his whole discussion of the Spirit. It seems to me that Paul clearly held that God gives the Holy Spirit to every believer *when he believes,* and that this giving of the Spirit marked the believer as belonging to God.

Dr. Gordon holds that as sinners receive Christ for justification, so those who have been justified or regenerated should receive the Spirit for sanc-

---

[1] *The Ministry of the Spirit,* p. 78.

tification.[2] To prove that receiving the Spirit is subsequent to receiving Christ, he refers to Paul's saying in Galatians 3:2.[3] Paul says to the Galatians, "Did you receive the Spirit by works of law or by the hearing of faith?" But this does not prove that Paul means that they received the Spirit apart from, and subsequently to, receiving Christ. Paul is speaking rather about receiving the Spirit when they received Christ. Dr. Gordon refers to the case of the disciples in Acts 19 to prove that one might be a disciple without receiving the Spirit. I take it rather that in Acts 19 Paul had these people baptized (or rebaptized, if you prefer) on the ground that if one did not know anything about the Spirit, he did not know Christ. In Paul's teaching, to receive Christ is to receive the Spirit. There is no reception of the Spirit apart from receiving Christ, either at the time of conversion or later. Receiving Christ is receiving the Spirit.

As for receiving Christ for justification and then receiving the Spirit for sanctification in a separate transaction, we need to remember two or three things. One is that in the teaching of Paul, of John, and of the New Testament as a whole, there is only one object of faith. That object of faith is Christ or God revealed in Christ. There are not two objects of faith, one Christ and the other the Holy Spirit. God as revealed in Christ is the one object of faith, and the Holy Spirit is everywhere the power working in us to enable us to exercise faith in Christ. As pointed out in our Introduction, Christ furnishes the objective factor in religion, the Holy Spirit the subjective. We trust in Christ,

---

[2] *Ibid.*, pp. 68-69. See his whole chapter on "The Enduement of the Spirit."
[3] *Ibid.*, p. 71.

and the Holy Spirit is the power enabling us to trust. To make Christ the object in one act of faith, and the Holy Spirit the object in a separate act of faith looks too much like tritheism. This is not Paul. As to sanctification, Paul's main use of this term is not something subsequent to justification. Paul uses sanctification in the main as another way of describing what takes place when one becomes a Christian. In Paul's usage, all Christians are saints or sanctified persons.

This by no means signifies that one should not receive the Spirit in fuller measure subsequently to justification. He should. And oftentimes a Christian or a church or other group of Christians should go through a great crisis in which, by the power of the Spirit, he (or they) is lifted to a higher plane in the Christian life. No doubt Protestant Christianity has talked so much about sanctification as a progressive work of grace subsequent to justification or regeneration that we have overlooked the possibility and the need for such radical changes in the Christian life. This progressive development has often been taken for granted as almost an automatic and necessary thing. This is not true. And many Christians need to be brought to realize that it is not true. I am not arguing against the need and possibility of a deeper experience of the Spirit, either as a progressive matter or as something that may come in a great crisis. What I am arguing against is that it is something that comes *in vacuo,* as something apart from our relation to Jesus Christ. And if a Christian realizes the need of such a deeper experience of the Spirit, what he needs to do is to examine himself in relation to Christ and his service. And if he will give himself more fully to Christ and let Christ more fully master his life, he will receive a deeper measure of the Spirit.

As to the sealing of the Spirit, I am fully convinced that what Paul means by this is the impartation of the Spirit to those who believe in Christ, *when they believe in him.* When one believes in Christ, God imparts his Spirit to such a one, as a permanent matter. This is what constitutes one a Christian, as already pointed out.

Paul uses another term to express this idea. He speaks of the "earnest" of the Spirit. In 2 Corinthians 1:22, he says that God sealed us and gave us the earnest of the Spirit (cf. Ephesians 1:14). This word translated earnest means pledge money. It is a down payment to guarantee that one will not go back on a promise that he has made to pay a larger sum. It is a forfeit that one gives to pledge himself to complete a transaction.

Another expression that Paul uses in line with this thought is the word "first fruits." The first fruits were a promise of the coming harvest. Two things were involved in the offering of the first fruits. One was that the coming harvest would be of the same nature as that which was brought into the Temple. The other thing was that the first fruits were just the beginning of the harvest. God's Spirit dwelling in us is the promise of a larger harvest to come. We have had only a foretaste of what God will do for us in Christ. Also, what God will do for us in the future will be of the same nature as that which he has already done.

If one is inclined to listen to the criticism that is sometimes hurled at religion, namely, that it is a scheme of the priestly class or of the capitalistic class to keep people satisfied with the conditions under which they have to live here and now with the promise that they shall eat pie in the sky by and by, then let him read Romans 8:18-25, and let him experience something of the power of the Spirit in his own heart. In that case, he will never again be satisfied with himself or with the world in which he lives. But his main discontent will be with himself and the world because of its moral and spiritual corruption; and he will realize that the only power that can bring final and complete deliverance to himself and to the whole creation is the power of God himself dwelling in his people and his world and working toward his goal of ultimate redemption. The indwelling Spirit will give him a definite and well-grounded hope of ultimate, personal deliverance; and Paul seemed to look for a final transformation of all things in line with the purpose of God.

We see, then, that the Spirit of God abiding in our hearts is the assurance to us of our complete salvation. The Spirit makes us yearn for complete deliverance from sin and all its evil effects. Moreover, it is through the Spirit that the suggestion comes from Romans 8:11 that life will be given to our mortal bodies. Paul says that if the Spirit of him who raised Christ Jesus from the dead dwells in us he will also make alive our mortal bodies through his Spirit that dwells in us.[4]

So far we have seen that Paul makes the indwelling Spirit the mark of a man's being a Christian. The Spirit of God in a man means that God is taking possession of a man's life and marking that life

---

[4]The text here may be *because of* his Spirit. In either case the meaning would be about the same. The Spirit that began our salvation will complete it.

as his. The suggestion is contained in Ephesians 1:14 that God is now taking control of that which is his own possession. Perhaps the thought is that God purchased us by the blood of Christ; now he is taking over what is his. The Spirit thus signifies three things in relation to man's salvation. The possession of the Spirit constitutes one a Christian. The Spirit also gives a consciousness of sonship to God. In the third place, the indwelling Spirit is the assurance of our final and complete deliverance from sin and corruption.

CHAPTER VII

THE TEACHING OF PAUL
(Continued) :

The Holy Spirit and Efficiency in the Christian Life

We will now turn our thought in a little different direction. Let us consider some respects in which Paul indicates that the Spirit makes the Christian life efficient.

We might begin with Paul's statement in 1 Corinthians 12:3. Paul says that no man can call Jesus Lord except in the Holy Spirit. No man can know Jesus as Lord except as the Holy Spirit enables him to see and realize the fact.

A man's efficiency in the Christian life depends on the extent to which Jesus Christ becomes the Master of his life.[1] Efficiency in the Christian life depends on the extent to which Christ dominates one's life. But it is only as the Spirit takes possession of us that Christ can master us. It is in and through the Spirit that Christ takes possession of us. Here we have a general statement that will be seen now in several of its phases.

I

This thing of living a Christian life has been (and still is) too much a matter of obeying or follow-

---

[1] This thought, I believe, goes back to Augustine.

ing a Christ who lived centuries ago. We were supposed to know about him (hardly to know him) by reading about him in the New Testament—his life, teachings, death, resurrection, and ascension. By this reading we were supposed to discover what it was to be a Christian, and then we were supposed to follow the program laid out for us. This was too much a matter of remote control. Oftentimes (shall we say, in most instances?), it was a matter of no control. One was supposed to derive certain principles from reading the New Testament which he should apply to his own life and the life of others. In most instances it was even more remote than that. One belonged to an ecclesiastical organization that somehow claimed the authority of the historic Christ for what it did. The officials of this organization— priests, bishops, pastors, or whatnots—spoke for the remote historical Christ, interpreting his will to the laity, the members of the church. One would not want to say that all this was useless. But what I am affirming is that it is not sufficient. To be what he can and should be in the lives of men, Christ must be real to them in an experience of immediate apprehension of him as a *living* Saviour. We have talked to men too much about an abstract system of doctrine or ethical principles of conduct. Sometimes we have boiled these principles down to certain ideas which we called the essence of Christianity. We need to bring ourselves under the control of a *living* Person, Jesus Christ, made available to us in an immediate experience of transforming power. This can only be done by the Holy Spirit. To bring us under the control of the living Christ is the function of the Spirit.

II

One thing that Paul says that the Spirit does for us is to reveal to us the truth. In 1 Corinthians 2: 6ff., Paul talks about the wisdom that had been hidden with God, which the rulers of this world had not known. Had they known it, he says they would not have crucified the Lord of glory.

He quotes from Isaiah about things which eye saw not, and ear heard not, and which entered not into the heart of man, the things which God prepared for them that love him. Sometimes preachers have taken this as a text from which to preach on the knowledge that we will have in the next life in contrast with what we do not know and cannot discover here. But this misses Paul's point. His contrast is not between what we know (or do not know) in this life in comparison with the next life. It is a contrast between what the world by its wisdom fails to discover and what God reveals by his Spirit. After stating that the rulers of this world had not known these things, he says, "But unto us God revealed them by his Spirit" (v. 10).

In the verses following (10b-16), Paul explains why it is that we can know these things only through the Spirit. He says that only the Spirit of man which is in him can understand the things of a man. Man's self-consciousness alone knows human life. No other form of life can penetrate the inner realities of man's life. It has to be known from the inside if known at all. In a similar way, the inner realities of the divine life can be known only by the Spirit of God and by those to whom the Spirit reveals them. Thus only those who have the Spirit of God have an understanding of divine things. But by the Spirit they are revealed to us so that we may know them. We see, then, that we are utterly dependent on the Spirit for the apprehension of spiritual truth. The natural (Greek psychical) man cannot receive these things. They can only be imparted to us by the Spirit of God.[2]

Without such a spiritual apprehension of truth there can be no growth in the Christian life. Paul goes on immediately after this (1 Corinthians chap. 3) to rebuke the Corinthians for being "carnal," babes in Christ, rather than full-grown Christians. He tells them that they still have to be fed on milk. They still are nourished on baby food. They are not spiritually mature Christians. They cannot eat meat. They have no power of spiritual digestion.

III

The Spirit inspires and guides the Christian's prayer life.

The outstanding passage on this point is Romans 8:26-27. Just preceding this, Paul has spoken of the whole creation as groaning and travailing in pain together and of Christians as travailing in pain together waiting for the adoption, the redemption of their bodies. He goes on to say in verse 26 that in like manner (as he gives hope of final deliverance from sin and corruption) the Spirit helps our infirmity. He makes clear what our infirmity is. It is that we do not know how to pray as we ought. The expression might mean what to pray for as we ought.

---

[2]Cf. what John's writings say about the Spirit of truth as he reveals Christ to men (John 14:25-26; 15:26; 16:13-15) and the anointing of the Spirit as giving an understanding of truth (1 John 2:20-21). Also, see what Hebrews says about knowing the Lord in the forgiveness of sins under the new covenant (Heb. 8:10-11).

I rather think the proper translation is how to pray, but that in meaning it covers the idea of what to pray for. Anyway, our infirmity is that we do not know how to pray as we ought, and the expression "as we ought" means *as it is necessary*. It is necessary that we should pray in a certain manner if we are to be heard. God does not hear just any kind of a prayer. And within ourselves we cannot pray as it is necessary for us to pray if we are to be heard.

The Spirit meets that situation. He lays hold to help us. The word translated "helpeth" is a compound made up of three parts. It means to *lay hold—over against—with*. The Spirit comes over against us, to lay hold with us, to help us. He supplies what we need but cannot furnish.

The intercession that he makes for us is not intercession far away in heaven or some distant place. It is intercession in our own hearts. His intercession is not intercession apart from our desires, longings, and pleadings. It is in and through these. These desires, pleadings, longings, are not what they should be. They may not take the right direction. Sometimes they do not take any direction. They may lie prone upon the earth. They do not rise and soar. Our hearts may be cold and listless. There may be little desire or disposition to pray. But as one waits on the Lord, there comes stealing into the Christian's heart longings and yearnings that he cannot express. He would utter them if he could. But they are too deep, too intense to express. At times the Christian can only groan, wishing that he could say what is in his soul. But he cannot.

Now this unutterable longing in the Christian's soul is the longing of the Spirit of God. It is created and guided by the Spirit. The Spirit gives it efficacy.

As the Christian thus prays under the tuition of the Spirit, Paul indicates that God searches his heart and sees that he prays according to the will of God (literally, according to God). Since the Christian thus prays according to the will of God, God can and does answer his prayer. It is only the Spirit-inspired and Spirit-guided prayer that God hears and answers.

Somene might be tempted to say that this makes the Christian only a tool in the hands of God and makes prayer a mechanical thing. Just the opposite is true. The test of a truth like this is experience and experience shows that it makes prayer a vital and creative thing. It is the creative Spirit of God who works in the Christian. Prayer is empty and mechanical, at best a matter of habit, form, or rote, without the Spirit.

We have the same thing here that we have everywhere in Paul's teaching concerning the Christian life—the initiative of God. God moves first and man responds. All the way through, God moves first. Not only does God move first, but it is he that sustains, guides, and gives efficiency to man's activity. One of the most definite statements about the human and divine in their relations is in Philippians 2:12-13. He says, "With fear and trembling, work out your own salvation; for it is God that energizes in you to will and to do [energize] on behalf of his good will." Here we have the same ideas concerning God and his activity in the Christian life as we have in Romans 8:26-27 concerning prayer. It might clarify the matter of prayer to look at this passage Philippians 2:12-13. Paul does not in the Philippian passage mention the Spirit, but he does speak of God as working or energizing in us. That, for Paul, means the work of the Spirit.

Notice the same divine initiative. It is God's own good pleasure that he is energizing in man to accomplish. He works in us to initiate and effect what he has planned. He wills the good before we do. Then he energizes to initiate the process (to will) and to carry through what he plans. But he does not complete the process without bringing man into active participation in the matter. Paul exhorts the Philippians to work out in their lives as God works in them. The word translated "work out" means to work out to completion, to finality. It means that they are to work out to expression what God works in them. It is worth noticing that while God initiates, he does not initiate the process and then quit—leaving man to complete the matter. God continues to work. He does not stop at any point in the process until the matter is complete. Religion is not a checkerboard affair in which God moves and then quits until man moves. God waits on man, but he does not quit. He waits, broodingly hovering over the sinner as he ponders and decides.

God works in and through the whole process, but man is not to be passive. We are not to say, "God works, therefore I quit." The proper inference is, "God works, therefore I work."

The same thing holds in prayer. The Spirit works in man. But man is not to be passive because God works. Man is to respond and respond actively. Man is not to assume the Quaker attitude of passivity. Man is to desire, to seek, to pray, to exercise his will in prayer. But God initiates and energizes in it all. Man is to submit to God's will and God's inner working in it all. As man thus submits and prays under God's leading, God's will is carried out and made effective in man's praying. Without the guidance of the Spirit, his will could not be effected in man's praying.

IV

The Christian's ethical life is developed in the Spirit.

We will take as our central passage on this point Ephesians 4:25-32. In this paragraph Paul is giving some ethical instruction and exhortation to his readers. He deals with some elementary but important matters in the ethical life. He exhorts them to tell the truth, to control their tempers, to be honest in their dealings, to use pure language that will be upbuilding to the hearers, to be kind and conciliatory in relation to others. In this passage we have exhibited one of Paul's characteristics as a teacher. He never teaches truth simply for the sake of an abstract system of truth. He is not interested in a system of truth after the manner of a philosopher who seeks a system for its own sake. Paul sets out truth for the sake of life. In that respect, he was always pragmatic in his method of dealing with truth. On the other side, Paul never gave an exhortation to right conduct without supporting his exhortation with truth. He based his exhortations on fundamental principles of Christian truth. Some Christian teachers and preachers set forth truth in such an abstract and impractical fashion that, as I heard an old gentleman once express it, to listen to them is like trying to eat fence rails chopped up. On the other hand, some who boast of being practical only succeed in producing a great stir and commotion. Paul always joined fundamental truth and right conduct. He based right conduct on Christian truth. He joined in vital union truth and conduct.

In the paragraph that we are considering, Paul bases his exhortation to right conduct on the truth that the Christian is sealed unto the day of redemption in the Holy Spirit.

It is the indwelling Spirit in which the Christian is sealed unto the day of redemption that constitutes the basis of Paul's exhortations concerning the Christian's ethical life. He exhorts Christians not to grieve the Holy S p i r i t in whom they are sealed. As a matter of experience, Christians are aware of the fact that, after they experience the renewing presence of the Spirit in their hearts ethical wrongdoing brings grief to them. To commit any of the sins against which Paul warns them here becomes a matter of sincere sorrow to the one committing the wrong. His conscience is so sensitized by the indwelling Spirit that any known deviation from the path of rectitude produces sorrow in the soul.

This sorrow over wrongdoing is not simply the sorrow of the one committing the wrong; it is the grief also of the Holy Spirit abiding in him. It is this indwelling Spirit that creates this sorrow. Notice that it is in his character as holy that Paul speaks of the Spirit here. As holy he lives in the Christian and seeks to create holiness in the believer.

As holy, this indwelling Spirit does two things for the Christian. In the first place, he creates an increasing sensitiveness in the Christian's heart to sin. He gives an increasing maturity of judgment as to what is right and what is wrong. Along with this he makes one increasingly sensitive to the presence of wrong in one's life and conduct. This is the reason that in some cases the deepest confession of sin comes in mature Christian life rather than at the beginning.

The second thing that the Spirit does for the Christian is to give an increasing ability to overcome sin when recognized in one's life. The Christian needs the ability to discern the right and wrong and also the power to overcome the wrong when it is recognized. The Christian's greatest need ethically is a sufficient dynamic to overcome sin when it is recognized. Sometimes we think that only God's power can make us Christians, but that after that we must overcome in our own strength. That is altogether wrong. We can no more conquer sin in our own strength after we become Christians than we can make ourselves Christian at the first. The great need of Christians today and all the days is some power to lift them out of themselves, out of their selfishness, pettiness and sins, and transform their lives. According to Paul, the Holy Spirit is the power adequate to that task if we yield ourselves to his leading.

Evidently Paul believed that a religious foundation was necessary for man's ethical life. He would not have agreed with those modern philosophers[3] who hold that ethics should be independent of religion, that ethics should stand on its own feet. Paul evidently did not believe that man's ethical life could be divorced from religion.[4] Paul did not believe that man's ethical life could be divorced from religion because he did not believe that man was self-sufficient. He believed that man was a created and dependent being, that he was dependent on God in every phase and relation of life. He believed, furthermore, that man was a self-centered and,

---

[3]Not always professional philosophers, of course. Practically every man has his philosophy of life. Sometimes I am inclined to agree with G. K. Chesterton, that a man's philosophy of life is the most important thing about him.

[4]For an excellent discussion of this question, see *The Predicament of Modern Man*, by D. Elton Trueblood.

therefore, a sinful being and that only the Spirit of God in man could set one right with his fellow men. According to Paul, only the presence of the divine in him as holy love could make men in love serve one another.[5] The close connection between the indwelling Spirit and man's ethical life in Paul's thought is shown in 1 Corinthians 6:18-19. He warns his readers to flee fornication and grounds his warning in the fact that the Holy Spirit dwells in the Christian and thus constitutes his body a temple of the Holy Spirit. The Christian who commits fornication sins against his own body as the temple of God and against the Lord who bought him and dwells in him.

Another passage that shows the intimate relationship in Paul's mind between ethics and religion is Romans 1:18-32. Here Paul says that the invisible and eternal God has revealed himself through the visible universe, through the things that are made. But he shows also that men universally have rejected this knowledge of God which leads to the degradation and perversion of religion, leading to all kinds of idolatry. As a consequence of the perversion of religion, men were plunged into moral degradation. Men were corrupted in their ethical lives as a result of a perverted form of religion. I think it would represent Paul to say that only the indwelling power of God's Holy Spirit that would cleanse and purify the moral nature of man would set him right in his ethical relations and activities. We have the same connection of ideas in Ephesians 4:17-24. A little later he says that Christians should not be drunken with wine, wherein is riot, but be filled with the Spirit (Ephesians 5:18). Passages on this line could

---

[5] See Gal. 5:13 and context.

be multiplied, but these are suffiicient to show that Paul considered that the only hope for man's ethical life was in the indwelling Holy Spirit. This Spirit, if given right-of-way, renews, recreates man's moral nature, makes one quick to recognize the distinction between right and wrong, and gives a sufficient dynamic to do the right and overcome the wrong.[6]

What we have been discussing as the relation of the Spirit to the ethical life is what Paul in places calls sanctification—sanctification in the ethical sense. Paul's predominant use of the verb to sanctify and the noun sanctification is with reference to the initiation of the Christian life. But he also uses these with reference to ethical purity on the part of the Christian in his daily life. If anybody should think that Paul was an impractical idealist, he could not miss it worse. Paul insisted on moral living on the part of his converts and offered the power of the Spirit as the hope of their being able to do so in the midst of pagan society. The tide was evidently against uprightness and purity of life in such communities as Corinth. Immorality even crept into the churches founded and nourished by Paul (1 Corinthians chap. 5). Paul insisted strenuously on sanctification as over against impurity, especially sexual immorality (Romans 6:19-23; 1 Thessalonians 4:1-8; 5:23; 2 Thessalonians 2:13). In the passage in Romans, he insists that one cannot serve two masters; he cannot be the slave of both sin and righteousness. To serve sin means death; to serve God and righteousness means sanctification and eternal life. In Galatians 5:19, after enumerating the

---

[6]For a helpful discussion of ethics from a Christian point of view, see *The Christian Method of Ethics*, by Henry W. Clark, published by Revell. See also *Paul the Mystic*, by James M. Campbell, and *The Christ of Every Road*, chap. XXI, by E. Stanley Jones, published by the Abingdon-Cokesbury Press, 1930.

works of the flesh, he solemnly warns that those who practice such things shall not inherit the kingdom of God. In 2 Thessalonians 2:13, he tells us that sanctification is in the Spirit.

V

The Christian graces are the fruit of the Spirit.

This is really a continuation of the point just discussed with reference to the Christian's ethical life. But it is also an extension of the idea there discussed. There we started our discussion from the point of view of man's relations and conduct toward his fellow man. Here we are thinking, first of all, of the Christians's character and of that character as Christian. In thinking of ethical relations and conduct, we think of man's will and moral responsibility. In thinking of the graces of character, we think more of what Paul calls the fruit of the Spirit—the graces of character that naturally result from the indwelling and control of the Spirit.

Yet we must not separate these too sharply. They cannot be separated, though there may be a relative distinction; but we must keep in mind that character and conduct go together. Character expresses itself in conduct, and conduct helps to form character.

Our main passage is Galatians 5:17-26. In this passage, Paul contrasts life in the flesh and life in the Spirit. These, he says, are contrary the one to the other. They represent different types of living. Paul sets out the works of the flesh, and over against these he puts the fruit of the Spirit. It is important to keep in mind the main terms of two opposing systems as Paul puts them over against each other. These two systems, with their main terms, are: law—works—sin (flesh)—death; grace—faith—Spirit—

life. When we see any of these main terms, we should understand that the others are implied. Paul's most extended statement of these two contrasting systems is found in Romans 7 and 8; chapter 7 being in the main a graphic depiction of the law system with its consequences, chapter 8 a discussion of life in the Spirit. These will be treated more fully later.

Here in Galatians 5:17-26, we have the two systems contrasted in a brief but forceful manner under the terms "works of the flesh" and the "fruit of the Spirit." They are contrasted with reference to their results in life here and now. We have this contrast stated in briefer form in terms of the ultimate results on each side in the next chapter (6:7-8). Paul warns the Galatians that God is not mocked. Whatever a man sows, that shall he also reap. He that sows to the flesh shall of the flesh reap corruption; he that sows to the Spirit shall of the Spirit reap eternal life.

By the flesh Paul means unrenewed human nature. It is human nature out from under the control of the Spirit of God. It is not the material substance of the body as such. By the flesh Paul does not mean material substance but an ethical tendency or power. He does not regard matter as evil within itself. That idea comes from Greek philosophy, not from the Bible. In places, at least, Paul uses the term flesh as denoting the sin principle in man. But it is the sin principle as active. It works, it energizes. It works against the Spirit. It divides a man so that he cannot do what he would (v. 17c; cf. Romans 7). The only way to be freed from the enthralling power of the flesh is to let the Spirit take over the reins of one's life. If we are led by the Spirit, we are not under law (v. 18). If we walk by the Spirit, we will not complete the desire of the flesh.

When Paul talks about the works of the flesh, it sounds to me as if he might be thinking of something artificially produced, something abnormal, something alien to man in his true estate, something that is an intruder in life that is genuinely human.[7] On the other side, Paul speaks of the fruit of the Spirit. Possibly the singular fruit implies the unity of the Christian character produced by the Spirit. The word "fruit" also suggests that the qualities here named are the natural result of the working of the Spirit in us. These qualities are not something artifically produced; they are the inevitable result when the Spirit of God controls the inner life of man. Paul says that against these qualities there is no law. When love, joy, peace, longsuffering, kindness, goodness, faithfulness, meekness, self-control, take charge of a man's life, he needs no outside authority to control him; he controls himself in the Spirit. The Spirit brings man to his true self. Modern man is seeking—clamoring, one might almost say—for autonomous self-control. His big mistake is that he thinks that to be his true self, he must shut God out. Just the opposite is true. To be his true self, he must let God in. God in Christ is the true creative power in man that brings man to himself, to his true ideal. Here we have in these Christian qualities the refined fruit of Christian character. Of course, there is no law against such. Law, Paul says, is for evildoers (1 Timothy 1:9). Law is an external, restraining power that seeks to compel one to do the right. Law is not needed where one, of his own volition, as a spontaneous expression of his inner life, does the right thing. This seems to be Paul's meaning when he says that, if one is led by

----

[7]This is true, whether Paul meant to imply it in this statement or not.

the Spirit, he is not under law (v. 18). Such a person does not need to be under any kind of coercive restraint. The inner compulsion of the Spirit leads him to do right. To do right is the natural and inevitable expression of the life of the Spirit in his inner nature.

One needs to be careful about pressing an analogy from nature too far in the spiritual and ethical realm, but perhaps it is not going too far to see in the expression "fruit of the Spirit" the idea that these ripened qualities of Christian character do not come so much by man's striving and energizing as they do by yielding oneself to the Lord. The Spirit takes possession of the yielded life. Experience is a factor in developing these qualities, usually, I should say, an essential factor. But the power that produces these qualities is the power of the Spirit, not the power of man seeking to cultivate these qualities by the energy of his own will. The life must be yielded. As previously pointed out, however, this is not to be taken in the sense of passivity. The yielded life can be, will be, in fact, if yielded in a true and understanding sense, an active life. To claim to yield one's life without engaging in active service may be an evasion rather than a true yielding. But my conviction is that modern Christians need to learn to be still and know that the Lord works. One may even try to serve God in the energy of the flesh. Paul says that if we live in the Spirit we should also walk by the Spirit (v. 25). Our lives should be yielded to the Spirit. He will give us life; he will develop in us the graces of Christian character; he will direct us in an active walk for Christ.

It is interesting to notice on this question of Christian character how Paul's picture of the Chris-

tian man and his virtues corresponds to the character of Jesus as depicted in the Gospels. Jesus, in
setting out the qualities required by citizenship in
the kingdom of God, really gives a picture of himself. Paul also delineates the character of Jesus
in telling us about the graces of character produced
in the life of the believer by the Spirit. This shows
two things. One is that Paul really knew the Jesus
of history as he lived and worked among men. By
some means, doubtless through the testimony of eye
witness, Paul knew quite intimately the character
of Jesus.[8] It shows also that Paul's conception of
the divine Spirit and his work was not that of an
emotional orgy but was moral and ethical. Paul was
no wild enthusiast. His religion always had at its
center the element of rational and moral control.
Christian character and conduct were the fruit of
the Spirit. The Spirit was the Spirit of Jesus.
History and experience were joined in the Spirit. The
experience of God in the Spirit was one with the
revelation of God in the Jesus of history. The two
factors—the historical and the experiential—formed
a unity.

VI

The Spirit bestows freedom on the believer.

Paul's letter to the Galatians is a polemical tract
in favor of spiritual freedom. Paul had planted the
gospel in Galatia. Following on his heels, the Judaizers had told the Gentile converts that it was not
enough for them to believe in Jesus, that faith in
Jesus alone would not save. It would be necessary
for them, in addition, to be circumcised and keep the
Jewish law. No doubt these Judaizers told them that

---

[8]See *The Mind of Christ in St. Paul*, by Frank Chamberlin Porter, **pp.
17ff.**

it was all right to believe in Jesus, but that they should not stop with that. They must go all the way and become Jews in their religion.

Here was Paul's major theological battle. And it is important to notice that it was a battle in theology. No man who was uncertain in theology could have met this issue. Paul was not uncertain in theology. On many things Paul was willing to compromise. He became all things to all men that by all means he might save some (1 Corinthians 9:22). But Paul was thoroughly convinced that in this matter the gospel itself was at stake. He calls this another gospel. He believed that this was no gospel (Galatians 1:6-10). This to him was a perversion of the gospel.

I have heard men say that Paul taught that a man should have faith to be saved, but that Paul did not say that faith and faith alone would save. But if I understand Paul in Galatians and Romans—in all his writings, in fact—that is exactly what Paul did teach. He taught that nothing outside of faith in Christ was necessary to salvation. That was his main contention against these men who were trying to win his converts away from faith in Jesus Christ to an effort to keep the Jewish law for salvation. And Paul was in dead earnest. Into that fight Paul put everything that he had. It was no half way matter with him. To his mind, to give up faith in Christ for the Jewish law was to surrender the gospel entirely: it was to fall away from grace. It was to give up freedom in the Spirit for bondage under the law.

It was being decided at that time whether the new movement going back to Jesus was to be a form of Judaism or whether it was to be an independent movement that would stand on its own feet. **Paul** makes it clear in Galatians that going to circumcision and the law was a form of bondage in religion. Christ had set men free.

Go back to what we have previously mentioned: that Paul puts over against each other two systems.[9] One system is a system of grace and faith, the other of works and law. The main terms in one system are: law—works—sin (flesh)—b o n d a g e—death. On the other side are: grace—faith—redemption (Spirit)—freedom—life. Paul does not always state either system in exactly the same terms; that is, he does not always bring to the front the same features of the system. But the salient features on each side are clear. And the contrast between the two is always sharp and definite. One system gives freedom; the other brings bondage.[10] According to Paul, a religion of bondage is not always one of low moral ideals or one of superstitious views of the spiritual world. At times he seems to be writing with such an elementary and superstitious system in mind. At times he seems to be reminding his Gentile converts that they came from such an evironment and contrasts the freedom of the gospel with their former condition. (Cf. 1 Corinthians chap. 8; Galatians 4:8ff.) It is not these superstitious and idolatrous religions, however, with which Paul contrasts the gospel with its freedom. He contrasts the gospel usually with the law and its doctrine of one God and its exalted moral ideal and its demand for absolute obedience. In other words, Paul did not usually contrast the gospel with its freedom in the

---

[9]And in the last analysis there can be only two. Every system that has any definite conception of God must hold that men are acceptable to him either on a basis of grace and faith or law and works.

[10]Cf. Jesus, according to the Fourth Gospel. See John 8:34-36.

Spirit with the lowest in religion of that day; but he set this gospel over against the best in the way of religion and shows how the gospel meant freedom, and the best outside the gospel meant bondage. Paul knew the system of Judaism. He had been brought up in the Jews' religion and had been zealous in promoting it before he met Christ on the Damascus road. He was proud of this religion. He was proud of belonging to the strictest sect of that religion—Pharisaism. But when he came to see this system in the light of Christ, he came to realize that adherence to it meant spiritual bondage and could mean nothing else.

When Paul spoke of bondage under the law, he spoke out of experience. The contrast between bondage under law and freedom in Christ is set out in Romans 7 and 8. Chapter 7 is probably the record of Paul's experience as a Pharisee, but it is his experience looked back on through Christian eyes.[11] It is the experience of a man who knows what it means to be delivered by the power of the Spirit.

The contrast might be stated as life in the flesh and life in the Spirit. In 7:5, Paul says that when we were in the flesh, the passions of sins which were through the law wrought in our members to bring forth death. The rest of chapter 7 seems to be a development of the implications of this statement. It is the development of what life in the flesh means.

One thing involved in life in the flesh as Paul reflects on his experience under the law is that the law intensifies sin. It brings it out into the light so that the law gives a knowledge (ἐπίγνωσις), a clear and definite knowledge, of sin (Romans 3:20). But I am convinced that Romans 7 means more than

---

[11]Cf. James Denny in *Expositor's Greek Testament*.

that. The law does more than reveal the sinfulness of sin. It actually aggravates sin. By means of law, sin becomes transgression—wilful violation of known law. The law said, "Thou shalt not covet." But that did not keep Paul from coveting. The commandment was the occasion for sin's coming alive. It sprang up and became active and aggressive. As Paul struggled to overcome this hostile power within him, as he struggled to do the thing that he recognized as right, he found himself helpless in the grasp of this hostile power. It would seem as if Paul at first thought of the law as a power hostile to him and seeking to enslave him.

He does find himself enslaved, but he does not charge it to the law in the sense of making the law evil. He charges it rather to the "flesh", or sin dwelling in him. The law is holy and righteous and good. Ideally, it was meant to bring life, but actually it brings bondage and death. It deceives Paul by making him think that it meant life when actually it brought death. This was due to the fact that on account of "sin in him" or, the flesh, he could not obey the law. There was something in him that enabled him to recognize the right and strive to do the right, but he could not do what he would. He found himself divided against himself. Paul discussed the divided self before the modern psychologists did. Paul did not believe in total depravity in the sense that the unregenerate man had no good impulses, but he did in the sense that outside the grace and power of God man is entirely unable to deliver himself from the power of sin. If man were totally depraved in the sense that he had no impulses toward the right, that all of him was entirely bad, then it is doubtful if he could be saved. Would that not be the state that Jesus warned the Pharisees that they were in danger of coming into when they accused him of doing his works in the power of the devil? In that kind of a situation there would be nothing in man to which the gospel could appeal. This, Karl Barth holds, is the state of man before regeneration. He holds that the image of God in which man was created has been obliterated, that in man there is no connecting point for the gospel, that when Paul says that in Christ there is a new creation, he is speaking literally, that regeneration is a miracle of sheer omnipotent power.

This, it seems to me, is going too far. Dr. John Baillie concedes that God could regenerate an inanimate object or an animal.[12] I see no need of conceding any such thing. God can only regenerate man, not things or animals. There must be a natural basis on which to work before he can regenerate anything. Generation must precede regeneration. Creation must be the basis of the new creation.

But while Paul did not hold that man was totally depraved in the sense that he had no good desires or impulses, that he could not even desire or strive after the good, he did hold that man was so divided against himself that he could not achieve the good that he desired. He could desire and strive, but he could not crystallize the good into spiritual character. He could wish or will the good but he could not achieve it. The reason he could not achieve it was that his being was divided—part pulling one way, part pulling the other. The Greeks described this state as a man trying to ride two horses going in opposite directions. In order for man to be saved from this situation, the schism in his being, in his moral being,

---

[12]*Our Knowledge of God*, p. 21.

must be healed. This can take place only when man is unified in Christ. The only power that can heal this schism is the grace of God revealed and made available in Christ. The law cannot do it. The law can only condemn the evil; it cannot heal it. In striving to overcome the evil in himself, Paul finds himself helpless. He is enslaved. Finally he cries out in utter despair, "O wretched man that I am! who shall deliver me from the body of this death?" (v. 24.)

Spiritual bondage is thus an inner state of man. It is a state of division, frustration, helplessness. It is a state that man can produce, does produce, but it is a state that he can not remedy. Man can bring himself under the bondage of sin, but he cannot deliver himself from it. His will is not equal to the task, because his will is divided and frustrated. The will is only the man functioning to effect what he desires. When man sets before himself a desired end but cannot do what he would, he is frustrated and his moral nature is weakened. Man cannot deliver himself from such a state because it is his own frustrated state from which he needs deliverance. Help must come from without. It must come from a power greater than man; it cannot come from the law. The law can command; it can demand; but it cannot furnish the power to accomplish. The self must be unified and rectified.

When Paul utters his cry of despair quoted above, the next thing is a cry of thanksgiving, a shout of victory (v. 25). It is not the strength of man's will that gives the victory, but the victory does not come against his will. He must consent. He must come to the point of conscious helplessness and yield to God in Christ. Then victory comes. In chapter 8, Paul sets life in the Spirit in striking contrast to life in the flesh which he has just described in such graphic terms. In 8:2, Paul says that the law—the rule or control—of the Spirit of life—the Spirit that produces life—liberated him from the law—control or rule—of sin and death. The rule of sin and death has been driven out by a higher power, the Spirit that produces life and freedom. He tells how this was done. The thing that the law could not do, because it was weak through the flesh, God did by another method. The thing that the law could not do was to give victory over sin. God accomplished this end by sending his own son in the likeness of sinful flesh. Paul is saying here that Christ took flesh, but that it was not sinful flesh. He sent him for (περὶ) sin. Here we have the incarnation and atonement joined together, not separated. It took both to deliver from sin. In this way, he says that God condemned sin in the flesh. That does not mean atonement; that is in "for sin." By "condemned sin in the flesh" he means that he broke its power in human life. He gave man the power to conquer it. All this was in order that the righteous requirement (ordinance) of the law might be fulfilled in us who walk not after the flesh but after the Spirit.

The righteous requirement of the law was fulfilled in us in the sense that we were enabled to live up to what the law required. This means that man is not saved by being delivered from moral requirement but by being given the power to meet those requirements. The standard is not lowered. The standard of Christ is as high as that of the law in the Ten Commandments. But the man is given strength to meet progressively its requirements.[13]

---

[13]Cf. 1 John 5:3-5.

Paul goes on to talk about the mind of the flesh and the mind of the Spirit. The word translated mind means mind or thought, with the emphasis on the moral quality of the mind or thought. So victory comes by changing the inner man. We stated a little earlier that spiritual slavery was a matter of the inner state of the man. So is spiritual freedom. But this inner state of spiritual freedom is produced in man by the Spirit of God, not by the man himself. His spirit is set free, but set free by the divine Spirit. There are places where it is difficult to tell whether Paul means the spirit of man or the Spirit of God when he uses the word spirit. (See Romans 8:10.) But the two must not be identified. The Spirit of God which sets man's spirit free and sets it to singing[14] is the Spirit of God which is objective to man. This Spirit transforms man's whole inner life, makes him new, but is not man, nor is man to be identified with the Spirit.

The Spirit of God that brings freedom to man's spirit gives the consciousness of sonship and delivers from the bondage of fear. The consciousness of sonship to God and of being a joint-heir of all things with Jesus Christ gives a man the conviction that he need not fear the worst that the universe can do to him (vv. 14-17, 31). In the paragraph 8:18-25, Paul talks about the sufferings of this present life but points to the hope of final and complete deliverance. The Christian longs in his deepest being for deliverance from the bondage of corruption into the glorious liberty of the children of God. The Spirit within him is the ground of hope for such deliverance beyond death. Thus we see that the Spirit of God in man gives him victory over sin, transforming his inner

---

[14] See Eph. 5:18-20.

life and releasing redemptive and conquering power over the enslaving power of sin in him.

The external side of this matter is that Paul considered that men were enslaved by law and that only the redemptive work of Christ—that is, the power of the Spirit—could free them. The whole book of Galatians is a setting out of this matter. In Galatians, he argues with his converts to keep them from turning back to slavery. In the allegory of Sarah and Hagar, he sets over against each other the two systems, the gospel and freedom and the law and slavery (Galatians 4:21-31). Hagar represents Mount Sinai in Arabia and the Jerusalem that now is. She is in bondage with her children. But Isaac, who was the child of promise, represents the Jerusalem that is free. Here we have the gospel standing for freedom.

In places, Paul seems to consider the law as a standard of requirement. As seen in Romans 7 and Galatians 3:11-12, this brings condemnation, death, bondage. In other places, Paul seems to be thinking of the law as a ceremonial system. This also brings bondage (Galatians 4:8-11; Colossians 2:14-17). In Colossians, he exhorts them to let no man judge them in meat or in drink or in respect of a feast day or a new moon or a sabbath day. The ground of the exhortation is that Christ has blotted out the "bond written in ordinances that was against them." These, he says, are a shadow of things to come; but the body is Christ. Christ is the reality to which these things had pointed. Paul was afraid that his converts would become enslaved to the shadows rather than grasping the reality. Many forms of religion since, claiming to be Christian, have done just that.

As already indicated, in places Paul seems to be looking back on the vain religions from which his converts have been delivered. He reminds the Galatians that they had been in bondage to them that were no gods (4:8). He says in 1 Corinthians 8, in discussing the eating of meats offered to idols, that an idol is nothing in the world, and that there is only one God, the Father, of whom are all things; and one Lord, Jesus Christ, through whom are all things. Therefore, to Paul, eating meats sacrificed to idols is no worse than eating any other food. All food is to be received with thanksgiving as the gift of God. But, he says, not all men have that knowledge. If they eat, they would eat as a thing offered to idols. Their conscience would be defiled. Paul says, therefore, that he refrained from eating meat or from doing anything else that would offend the weaker brother. He recognizes that he who regarded the idol as anything would be the weaker brother, but Paul is willing to restrain his own liberty for the sake of the weaker brother for whom Christ died. This might look as if Paul were surrendering his freedom. I think it would be more in accord with Paul's thought to say that he regarded it as a part of his freedom to give up some of his personal rights for the sake of the other man. A Christian man is free to restrain his freedom for the sake of others.

It is quite evident that Paul's conception of spiritual freedom was quite radical. When the Spirit came in and took possession, Paul would say that, where the Spirit of the Lord is, there is liberty (2 Corinthians 3:17). He recognized only one Lord. He believed in giving his life over to that one Lord in the Spirit. He might be in a Roman jail but his spirit could sing a song of redemption. He might be in a storm at sea, but the Lord would stand by and give him cheer. The world can kill the body of such a man; it cannot enslave his spirit.

Spiritual freedom comes to the believer, Paul holds, because the believer becomes the slave of Christ and Christ excludes all rival powers from mastery over the Christian. He gives mastery over sin and over the law as an external and restraining power in the Christian's life. He gives deliverance from fear of what the world or any hostile powers, seen or unseen, may do to the believer.

CHAPTER VIII

THE TEACHING OF PAUL
(Continued):

The Holy Spirit and the Church

The Spirit constitutes the life and efficiency of the church.

In considering Paul's doctrine of the Spirit, we must give some attention to the work of the Spirit in relation to the church. We cannot properly understand Paul on either the doctrine of the Spirit or of the church without considering the relation of the two.

The fundamental matter in considering this relation is the fact of the indwelling of the Spirit in the believer. We have already seen that it is the incoming of the Spirit into the heart of the believer that constitutes him a Christian and gives him the consciousness of sonship to God. The indwelling of the Spirit, we have seen further, gives efficiency to the Christian's prayer life, in fact, his total life as a Christian. It is this indwelling Spirit that constitutes the hope of his final and complete deliverance from sin and evil and is the basis of the development of Christian character and moral life now.

I

It is this indwelling of the Spirit that gives the church its existence. Without the experience of the indwelling Spirit there could be no such thing as the Christian church. Perhaps a good place to begin our consideration of Paul's thought on this matter is with 1 Corinthians 3:16-17 and 6:19-20.

In each of these passages, Paul speaks of Christians as a temple (or sanctuary) of God. (Cf. also 2 Corinthians 6:16; Ephesians 2:20.) The context shows that it is the fact that the Spirit dwells in Christians that constitutes them a sanctuary of God. It is clear that Paul considers that the Spirit dwells in believers both individually and collectively. The word that he uses here for temple is instructive. It does not denote the whole temple structure. That was denoted by the word "ἱερον." This latter was the word used when it was said that Jesus went into the Temple and found those who sold oxen and sheep and doves (John 2:14; cf. Matthew 21:12ff.; Mark 11:15-17; Luke 19:45f.). This word denoted the whole Temple enclosure, including the court of the Gentiles. There was another word, "ναὸς," that was used for the inner sanctuary, composed of only the Holy Place where only the priests could enter (cf. Luke 1:9) and the Most Holy Place, where only the high priest could enter once a year on the great day of atonement with blood to offer for his own sins and the sins of the people. This second word, "ναὸς," is used in the New Testament in a figurative sense for both Christ and the church. In the Gospel of John, Jesus uses it for his body when he said to the Jews, "Destroy this temple [sanctuary,] and in three days I will raise it up" (John 2:19). It is used by Paul in the passages being considered here (1 Corinthians 3:16-17; 6:19-20). Jesus applies it to his own person as the place where God and man meet; Paul applies it to believers as the place where God dwells with his people. As to what Paul has in mind, the following passages in the Old Testament will furnish something of the background: Exodus 29:42-46; Leviticus 26:12-13; Ezekiel 37:27-28; Jeremiah 31:33-34. In the Old Testament, the tabernacle was the place where God promised to meet his people and dwell with them. He would be their God and they should be his people, with all that this relationship meant in the way of redemption and blessing. Paul emphasizes that if the Spirit of God dwells in his people, they are his habitation. In Ephesians (2:21-22), Paul says that believers are growing into a temple (ναὸς) in the Lord and being builded into an habitation of God in the Spirit. The Spirit of God dwelling in his people is the thing that makes them God's people, God's habitation. The passage in 1 Corinthians 6:19-20 shows that this indwelling of the Spirit has redemptive significance, for Paul goes on to remind them that they are not their own, for they have been bought with a price. (Cf. Exodus 29:45.)

All Paul's language in regard to the church is in harmony with the nature of the church implied when he speaks of the people of God as the temple or sanctuary of God. The church is God's habitation, God's earthly dwelling place. Both in the Old Testament and in the New, it was recognized that no house made by man could contain his presence, that heaven and earth were not sufficient for that. God dwells not in temples made with hands but in the hearts of his people. In the person of Christ, God came down to dwell with man. Christ was the incarnation of God. That is the reason Jesus speaks of his body as the temple (ναὸς) or sanctuary. He told the Jews that if they should destroy this temple, in three days he would raise it up. Now God is being reincarnated in his people. By his Spirit, he enters into them and dwells there.

In line with this thought, Paul calls the church the body of Christ (Romans 12:4-8; 1 Corinthians 12:12-31; Ephesians 2:22; 4:15-16). Christ is head and we are the members. The church is thus a living organism. It is not fundamentally an organization. It is a living something. An organization may be dead and mechanical. The church is vital. A man cannot in reality be a member of the church of Christ unless he is made a member of the body by the indwelling Spirit of God. Christ is the life of the church as well as its head, and he is the life of every real member of the church. A man cannot be a living member of the body of Christ unless Christ lives in him by his Spirit. Paul, in one place, speaks of the body as having many members and yet being one body, and then he says, "so also is Christ" (1 Corinthians 12:12). This language would seem to include the members of the body in the Person of Christ. Paul does make believers members of his body.

The fact that the church is constituted by the indwelling of the Spirit determines the nature of the church. It determines the nature of the church as a spiritual fellowship. The church is fundamentally the fellowship of the redeemed. It is the fellowship of those who have experienced redemption through faith in Christ as Redeemer and Lord. To say that the church is a spiritual fellowship might not be specific enough in view of the loose and general sense in which the word spiritual is sometimes used. The word spiritual in the New Testament, as well as in historical Christianity, is a redemptive term. It belongs to the family of terms associated with redemption in Christ, and it would be out of place if made to carry any other connotation or bear any other association. The Christian church, then, is not just any kind of spiritual association or fellowship. It is a fellowship of a very particular, spiritual type. It is a fellowship of redemption—a fellowship that grows out of an experience of being regenerated in Christ Jesus by the power of the Spirit.

The church, then, is not just a religious organization. There could be such a thing as a religious organization, with religious motives and purposes, without being a church. Whatever else would be necessary, it would have to be composed of the spiritually redeemed in Christ to constitute a Christian church.

The experience of redemption, of being spiritually renewed in Christ, *ipso facto*, brings one into the fellowship of the redeemed. The church universal is composed of the body of the redeemed living on earth at any particular time.[1] Christ is the head of this universal, spiritual body which draws its life and power from him in and through the Spirit (Romans 12:3-8; 1 Corinthians 12:12-31; Ephesians 2:21-22; 4:4-16). Paul applied the concept of the body of Christ both to the universal body, as just indicated, and also to the church located at a particular place. (See 1 Corinthians chap. 12.) This concept applies to the church at a particular place, however, as a fellowship of the redeemed rather than as an organization.

I am not trying to give a full definition of the Christian church. I am stating rather the fundamental nature of the church. What I say will apply to the church in the local or universal sense.

---

[1]Some would include the redeemed in heaven.

The church, then, is not primarily an organization, but a spiritual fellowship. Organization is distinctly secondary. I doubt if Paul or anybody else in New Testament times ever "organized" a church in anything like the modern sense of an organized church. What took place, it would seem from the record, is that Paul and others went into communities and preached. People were converted and just naturally got together and functioned as a spiritual fellowship or church. So far as there was organization, it was simple and subordinate. The extent and form of church organization should be determined by the nature of the church as a fellowship. Organization should be had only as the organization can be utilized to promote the ends of fellowship. Any organization, in nature or extent, that hinders fellowship should be omitted. Any that will promote fellowship should be effected. As indicated in the introductory chapter, organization may be substituted for spiritual life and power; organization may crush spiritual power.

II

Another phase of the matter is this. The spiritual nature of the church as a fellowship of the redeemed excludes an authoritarian organization of the church. To my mind, the fundamental cleavage among ecclesiologies today is along this line, and this cleavage goes back to conflicting views as to the nature of Christianity itself. One view regards Christianity as fundamentally a personal matter; the other regards it as fundamentally institutional. One considers that the primary purpose of Christ in his redemptive mission was to bring to the individual the redeeming love of God to be

accepted by an act of free choice. So far as the
church as an organization is concerned, it is a free
and voluntary association of redeemed individuals.
The other view is that Christ came primarily to
found an institution to whom he committed his
authority. This institution then communicates the
saving grace of God, under the delegated authority
of Christ, to other men. One view holds that every
man without the mediation of priests or sacraments
can go directly to the Lord himself and find forgiveness and spiritual blessings. One view is in
general the Protestant view, although some forms
of Protestantism are not any too clear and con-
sistent in holding to the view that every man can
come directly to God in Christ for himself. The
second view is in general the Catholic view (Roman, Anglican, and Orthodox). Schleiermacher
stated the two views about as follows: that in
Catholicism one gets to Christ through the church
while in Protestantism one gets to the church
through Christ.[2] One makes religion a free and
voluntary matter all the way through; the other
interposes priests and sacraments between the soul
and God. In one view, Christ bestows the Spirit on
the soul directly when one believes; the other holds
that the Spirit is mediated to the individual
through the church and her sacraments and min-
istries. One holds that the church is a fellowship in
the Spirit, expressed in a voluntary association of
free, redeemed persons; the other that the church
is an authoritarian institution mediating God's
mercy to individuals who are not competent to deal
directly with God in Christ for themselves. One
holds that each individual possessing the normal

[2]*The Christian Faith*, p. 103.

powers of human personality may know for himself through the indwelling Spirit, in a conscious
experience, the grace of God that saves and brings
assurance; the other makes the individual dependent on officials of the authoritative church for
a knowledge of God's mercy.

III

We turn now to another phase of the work of the
Spirit in relation to the church. So far, we have
tried to set forth the fact that the church as Christian is constituted as a fellowship by the redeeming
activity of the Spirit in the hearts of men. The
Spirit constitutes the church a spiritual fellowship
around Christ as the center. The Spirit also gives
efficiency to the worship and work of the church.
In other words, the indwelling Spirit enables the
church to function as a church. The church could
not exist without the Spirit. The church is his
creation. Likewise, the church cannot function as
a church except in and through the Spirit.

What is the function of the church? The function of the church is determined by its nature. Its
nature is that of a society of redeemed souls,
brought into fellowship with the living God and
with one another as redeemed souls. Its fundamental relationship as a society and as individuals
is with God in Christ. Its most important function
is to maintain unbroken, and develop this relation
to him as Lord and Redeemer. That means that
the most important business of the church is worship. To maintain direct and conscious relations
with Christ, the head and Lord of the church,
should be the main concern of every church. This
can be done only by the Spirit living in the church

and guiding in all its worship and activity. There may be variety as to forms of worship, but there must be no mistaking the fact that the church is dependent on the Spirit for the reality of its worship. The Spirit must release the springs of prayer and praise if there is to be genuine worship. The Spirit must create in the hearts and minds of the people the consciousness of God with all that that means. God in his love and holiness must be unveiled to the spiritual vision of men. Often men seek God for the sake of efficiency in evangelism, missions or social service. These forms of activity will certainly result when God is truly worshiped. But should God not be worshiped for his own sake? Should he not be worshiped and praised because he is worthy of our worship and our praise and not for what we may receive in return, even in the way of spiritual efficiency? God should be worshiped for his own sake and not for man's sake.

The individual Christian or a congregation of Christians maintains two relations or relations in two directions. One direction is perpendicular, the relation with God. The other is horizontal, the relation with fellow men. The relation with God is primary. A church is a congregation of those who have come into relation with God through an experience of his redemptive grace. Worship will keep this relation intact. It will open up the channels of intercourse with the heavenly world so that there will come fresh accessions of divine power into the hearts of the worshipers. The divine power thus coming into the hearts of men will express itself in horizontal directions. Worship will lead to service. Contact with God in worship, prayer, and praise will lead to service in evangelism and social activity of all kinds. There is a possibility of misinterpreting what was said above to the effect that God should be worshiped for his own sake, not for the sake of what we should receive. It might be put like this. Is true religion a matter of worship toward God or of service toward men? The answer is that it is both. Some men want to make it purely a matter of service toward man. Such people insist on a "practical" religion. They are impatient of a religion that does not show "results." They like to quote James about visiting the fatherless and the widows. American Christianity for the past third of a century or more has put the emphasis at this point. Along with pragmatism in philosophy, we have had a tendency toward a humanistic religion that was impatient with the idea of wasting time bothering about the unseen world. Such men have sometimes overlooked the fact that James said pure religion and undefiled *before God* was to visit the fatherless and widows and keep oneself unspotted from the world. Doing good to one's fellows is a part of religion. It is an essential part. But to leave out the Godward aspect is to leave out the primary thing in religion. It is to leave out the part that gives meaning and dynamic to all the rest. My conviction is that American Christianity is coming back to a deeper appreciation of the perpendicular aspect of religion.

IV

At the beginning of this section, we indicated two things about the Spirit in relation to the church. These were that the Spirit constituted both the life and the efficiency of the church. We saw that the indwelling Spirit constituted the very breath of life for the church; that the incoming of the Spirit producing a fellowship of redemption among men is the essence of the church. This, so we stated, determines the chief function of the church, which is worship. The Spirit of God as a conscious presence among men gives reality to worship and efficiency to service. As men worship God, as they keep in fellowship with him, the spirit of service is created in their hearts. There may be among men a certain disposition to benevolent activity without this conscious indwelling of the Spirit, but there is not likely to be the spirit of sacrificial, constant devotion to the welfare of mankind without this. Next to Jesus, we have no better example of this in Christian history than the apostle Paul. Never did any man devote himself to service to others more completely than did the apostle to the Gentiles. He says that it was the love of Christ that hemmed him in and pressed him on (2 Corinthians 5:14). This love of God is shed abroad in our hearts, he says, by the Holy Spirit which was given unto us (Romans 5:5).

In writing to the Corinthians, Paul has a somewhat extended discussion of what he calls spiritual gifts (*charismata,* charisms, gifts of grace) as they are related to the worship and work of the church at Corinth (chaps. 12-14).[3] Quite likely they had written Paul asking about the use of these gifts, especially, it would seem, the gift of tongues. At this distance, it is quite difficult, if not impossible, to make out with clarity all that Paul was try-

---

[3]These charisms, or spiritual gifts, are not to be identified with the gift or impartation of the Holy Spirit in regeneration. These spiritual gifts are not necessarily related to spiritual character. They may be temporary and are functional, designed to qualify one for service. The impartation of the Spirit to one when he believes constitutes him a Christian. It changes the fundamental spiritual character of the individual. The two—that is, God's giving of the Spirit to one so as to constitute him a Christian and these supernatural, spiritual gifts bestowed by the Holy Spirit—are not unrelated, but they are not to be identified.

ing to say. I am inclined to think that there are some details of Paul's discussion that will never be entirely clear to us. But the main lines are clear, and some of these we will note.

For one thing, Paul makes it clear that the Spirit was sovereign in the distribution of these gifts. They were gifts; they were not man's attainments. They were gifts of *grace*. Some modern men are very slow to admit that even the Lord, if they believe in any Lord, can give them any graces, assign them any functions, bestow upon them any powers, that are not their attainments. Paul is talking about *gifts of grace*. They were powers, functions, abilities that men did not attain; they were given to them. They were all given by the "same Spirit." They were ministrations of the "same Lord," workings, energizings of the "same God." And Paul says that all these gifts, the one and the same Spirit divided to each one severally as *he willed*.

A man's gift or function in the church and its work, then, did not depend on his choice or preference but on the sovereign will of the Spirit of God. God assigned to each man his gift and his work in relation to the church and its mission. This means that each man was to do his own work, perform his own mission, as it was assigned to him. Paul illustrates this by the members of the body. One member was not to be jealous of another. There could be harmony and efficiency only as each member did its own work without jealousy of the other. And each member of the body was to recognize the importance of its own work and, therefore, see that it was not neglected. The ear was not to say because I am not the eye, therefore I am not of the body; my work is of no importance. No matter how humble or insignificant any member's work might be, that member should recognize that it was necessary to the life and welfare of the whole. This means that every man should try to find out what his function in the life of the body is and try to do it in his way, not trying to do the other man's work nor in the manner of the other man. Each man should do his own work, in his own way, according to the will of God, and by the grace that God furnishes.

No man, therefore, should expect that all others should do their work like him. For instance, I have seen some preachers who seemed to think that if other preachers did not preach like them, they were not doing the thing right. A man should want to do the work that God has assigned to him and do it as God wants him to do it, not as the other man does. On the other hand, some seek to be original and only succeed in being queer. There is a difference between being original and being queer. A man, to be a success in the Lord's work, does not have to be either original or queer, but he does need to do the Lord's work as God meant for him to do it and not necessarily as the other man.

Another thing that comes out in Paul's discussion is that a man should exercise his gift for the good of the body as a whole and not for selfish ends. It would appear that some were desiring the more spectacular gifts, such as speaking in tongues. Spiritual gifts in the Corinthian church were quite varied. Some were more prominent than others and brought the recipient into more prominent notice. It is not quite clear just what speaking in tongues here was. It does not seem to be the same thing as it does in Acts 2. There the account would make the impression that it was preaching so that the people, gathered from over the Roman Empire, heard each one in his own language (Acts 2:6). However one may explain it, that seems to be what Luke means to say. But at Corinth, it is evidently different. In places, Paul talks as if it were some kind of ecstatic utterance between a man and God, perhaps having no rational significance to be grasped by the mind (chap. 14). In places, either the man speaking or someone else might be given the power of interpreting tongues. Then perhaps there might be a rational message derived from what was uttered. Paul makes it clear that there was no use in a man's talking before the church unless he could be understood. In places, Paul glories in visions, revelations, and what seem to be ecstatic experiences. But, in the last analysis, Paul put the emphasis on rational understanding and discouraged blind mysticism or irrational excesses. In one place, he seems to imply that confusion and emotional excess would drive people away from the gospel (14:23). All things were to be done unto edifying and in decency and in order. He says that the spirits of the prophets are subject to the prophets. A man did not have to let his emotions run away with him.

Paul did not seek dead uniformity in the church, but living unity. He recognized that there could be variety in unity and unity in variety. Nor did he put all gifts on a level of value. He did not absolutely forbid speaking in tongues, but he made it subordinate in value to prophecy. He did this on the ground that the intelligent was superior to the unintelligible. There was nothing in Paul's work to encourage the nonrational or uncontrolled emotions. He recognized the limitations of man's mind, but he did not discourage its use.

Paul puts among the Spirit's gifts to the church certain officials, or rather functionaries (1 Cor. 12: 28; cf. Ephesians 4:11 ff.). This could hardly be considered a list of officials to be maintained permanently in the churches. There is quite a difference between the statement in Corinthians and in Ephesians. Besides, in Corinthians, he passes from the persons exercising the function, such as apostles, prophets, and teachers, to miracles (powers, δυνάμεις, one of the words used in the New Testament for miracles), gifts of healings, helps, governments, kinds of tongues. In Ephesians, he confines himself to the persons, and represents them as the gifts to the church of the living, exalted Christ. Also, in Ephesians, he goes on to state at length that all these were for the perfecting of the saints, the building up of the body of Christ, and so on. He makes it clear that all gifts were for the service of the whole church, the maintaining of its unity, its protection from error, its upbuilding spiritually and ethically.

We have mentioned that Paul emphasized knowledge, spiritual understanding, and intelligence. How Paul would be shocked if he knew how his writings had been used to appeal to ignorance and prejudice in the name of spirituality! Paul did not believe that there was any contradiction between intelligence and spiritual power. He did denounce worldly wisdom of this age, knowledge that "puffed up" its possessor. Contrary to this kind of knowledge, Paul believed and emphasized spiritual intelligence that gave efficiency in the service of Christ. And he himself was the supreme exhibition of such spiritual intelligence.

V

But Paul's supreme emphasis was not on knowledge or intelligence. His supreme emphasis was on the ethical. It is instructive to notice that Paul puts his great discussion on love right in the center of his discussion of spiritual gifts. I doubt if Paul meant to class love as one of the charismata or spiritual gifts. I rather think that his language at the beginning of chapter 13 implies otherwise. In general, I think it would be true to say that spiritual gifts were temporary, given, at least at times, only for the occasion.

But Paul puts on the very pinnacle of God's gifts to man something permanent and enduring. Tongues, knowledge, and prophecy might pass away but love would not. Love is not something added to the man; love is a matter of character. Paul says in substance that the greatest thing that God does for a man is in the realm of character; it is to make him the right kind of a man.

Paul does not say in so many words that the love that he describes is divine love, but there would be no doubt in any man's mind on that question who reads about God's love manifest in the life of Christ, particularly if he had experienced the longsuffering, forgiving love of God in Christ. One who has read the life of Jesus and then reads Paul's description of divine love will readily see that the two match each other exactly. This love described by Paul is what Henry Drummond has called the greatest thing in the world. Indeed it is. It is the greatest thing in the character of God. John tells us that God is love (1 John 4:8, 16). And the greatest thing that the Spirit of God can do for a man is to transform him into the image of God as revealed in Christ. This love was shed abroad in our hearts through the Holy Spirit which was given unto us (Romans 5:5). When Paul speaks of the Holy Spirit as being given to us, he uses the aorist tense of the Greek verb, which indicates that it was a definite act and probably refers to the time of conversion. Then as the Holy Spirit lives in us and controls, divine love becomes the dominant quality in one's character. To make one that kind of a person is the greatest thing that God's Spirit does for his people.

CHAPTER IX

FIRST PETER, HEBREWS
REVELATION

So far, we have treated the main portions of the New Testament in their teachings concerning the Holy Spirit. We have considered the Synoptics, the book of Acts, John (Gospel, and First Epistle) and the Epistles of Paul (except the Pastoral Epistles). There are a number of the minor books that have little or no material on this subject. Here would fall James, Second Peter, Jude, and Second and Third John. We do need, however, to give some attention to First Peter, Hebrews, the Apocalypse and one or two statements in the Pastorals.[1] James says nothing about the Spirit and these others we are omitting contain practically no material on the subject.

I

In First Peter, we have a reference to sanctification in the Spirit (1:2; cf. 2 Thessalonians 2:13). Here we have nothing added to Paul's idea of sanctification.[2] In 1:11, Peter speaks of the Spirit of Christ that was in the prophets as testifying beforehand the sufferings of Christ and the glory that should follow. This expression, "The Spirit of Christ," doubtless refers to the Holy Spirit as working in the prophets and is thought of as the same Spirit who worked in and through Christ. The term

---

[1]In classing 1 Peter, Hebrews, and the Apocalypse as minor books, we mean with reference to the doctrine of the Spirit. In some other aspects they might not be so classed.
[2]See chap. VII, sec. IV, on Paul.

Christ is perhaps used here as a proper name for Jesus of Nazareth and not as a title (the Messiah).[3] When it is said that the Spirit testified beforehand the sufferings of Christ and the glory that should follow, this agrees with what we find in the Gospels. On the road to Emmaus, the risen Christ told the two disciples that it was necessary that the Christ should suffer and enter into his glory (Luke 24:24-25). So Peter gives us nothing essentially new. In the same connection, Peter refers (1:12) to those in his day who preached the good tidings in Holy Spirit sent forth from heaven. This again is reiterating what we have in Acts. This is the controlling thought of Acts—the witnessing of the disciples to Christ in the power of the Spirit.

One might see a reference to the Holy Spirit in 1 Peter 2:2,4 in which the author refers to "spiritual milk" as the nourishment of newborn babes, and to "a spiritual house" and to the offering of "spiritual sacrifices" to God. These, however, would be only indirect reference or implications as to the Spirit.

Again, in 3:18-19, Peter speaks of Christ as being put to death in the flesh and made alive in the spirit; and in 4:6, he says that the gospel was preached to the dead (those formerly living but now dead) in order "that they might be judged according to men in the flesh, but living according to God in the spirit." Since in each case the spirit is set in contrast to the flesh, the reference is probably not to the Holy Spirit but to the spirit of man or to the spiritual realm in general. So First Peter gives us little, if anything, new on the subject of the Spirit.

---

[3]See *Expositor's Greek Testament.*

II

In the book of Hebrews we have some material on the work of the Spirit. In this respect this book is different from Paul, especially in those places where Paul goes into experiential aspect of religion and the mystical dealings of God with man. There is little in Hebrews of Paul's or John's conception of union with Christ. We do have a suggestion of it in 6:4-5, where the author describes those who have been once for all enlightened, who have tasted of the heavenly gift, who were made partakers of the Holy Spirit, who tasted of the Word of God as good, and the powers of the age to come.

There is also in 8:8-12 and 10:16 an experiential knowledge of God in the forgiveness of sins under the new covenant as over against the old covenant in which the law was written on tables of stone. This is in line with what we have in John and Paul and other places in the New Testament, but does not add a great deal to our knowledge of the work of the Spirit beyond what we get from these other writings.

In another place a mystical tinge is given the author's thought. This is found in chapter eleven, the outstanding chapter on faith in the New Testament. Here the author regards faith as the power of the soul to appreciate and apprehend God and spiritual realities. Faith is the power to see, to lay hold of the spiritual world. As over against the natural senses by means of which we apprehend the natural or physical world, faith enables us to hold commerce with the spiritual world. Faith makes God and spiritual things real. It is only the man who is lacking in faith to whom God is unreal. By faith Moses saw him who is invisible. To Moses God was more real than Pharaoh and the riches of Egypt. While the Holy Spirit is not mentioned in this chapter, it is evident that the Spirit's work is distinctly implied in the vision of faith that brings a firsthand knowledge of God.

There is one passage often interpreted as referring to the Holy Spirit, but which is doubtful. This passage is 9:14. The author speaks of Christ as One who through eternal spirit offered himself to God for us. There is no article before the spirit in Greek. He does not say through *the* eternal Spirit, but through eternal spirit. The point he is making is that, in contrast to the blood of bulls and goats, the blood of Christ cleanses from sin effectively, so that the conscience is cleansed from dead works to serve the living God. These animal sacrifices are ineffective in comparison with the blood of Christ. He has just indicated that Christ procured for us "eternal" redemption. A little later he says that Christ is the mediator of a better covenant so that those who come to him may receive promise of the "eternal" inheritance. When he speaks of eternal redemption and eternal inheritance, he means a redemption and an inheritance that have the quality of finality, absoluteness about them. When he speaks of Christ as offering himself through eternal spirit, he is giving expression to the ethical quality of his offering as opposed to the offering of irrational animals for the sins of men. His offering is effective in that he offered himself. He offered himself through eternal spirit—in the spirit of absolute righteousness. In giving himself to death to save men, he brought to expression a spirit of goodness beyond which no quality of moral goodness can be conceived. In that sense it was eternal spirit.

It was moral goodness that had the quality of finality or absoluteness in it.

One of the best known passages in the book of Hebrews concerning the Spirit is found in 10:19. The author has set forth at length the blessings of the new covenant in contrast with the old. He has dwelt on the completeness and finality of the redemptive work of Christ. Christ has performed a once-for-all task in dying for the sins of men and opening up the way into the presence of God. There is no need or possibility of extending or duplicating that phase of his work. Moreover, he has entered into the very presence of God to make intercession for us. We can, therefore, enter into the Holy of Holies, into the very presence of God, assured of acceptance on the basis of his work for us.

The author makes a double application of the fact of the completeness of Christ's redemptive work. He says in 10:18 that there is no more offering for sins. But this fact means different things for different people. For those who accepted Christ and his offering for sin, it means grace and assurance. There is no more offering for sin. But the believer answers: "I need no other. His is enough. His offering is complete and sufficient. Why should I seek for another?" This is the answer today of the Christian to those who want to give us an eclectic religion, made up of elements from here, yonder, and everywhere. Some men want us to take the best from Buddhism, Mohammedanism, Judaism, Christianity, and all the other systems and put them together and thus make a system for ourselves. Moreover, every time the moon changed, they would want us to add a little from some other new system that had sprung up. The Christian's answer is:

"Why should I take a mixture of half-remedies when I have a complete and all-sufficient one already?" This author insists that Christ and his work are final and complete; no other remedy is needed. Beyond and except his there is no more offering for sin. But the Christian adds: "Thank God, no other is needed. His is final and complete." What the completeness of Christ's work for believers means the author sets out in verses 19-25.

But there is another side to the matter. This he sets out in verses 26-31. Some do not accept this offering made for sin. After receiving a full knowledge (ἐπίγνωσις) of this truth of Christ's redemptive work, they keep on (present tense in Greek denoting constant, habitual activity) willfully. They tread underfoot the blood of the covenant by which they are sanctified (provisionally and potentially) and do despite to the Spirit of grace. For them also there is no more sacrifice for sin. They have rejected the only real sacrifice for sin that there is. Consequently, they must suffer the consequences of their sins. Having rejected the all-sufficient sacrifice for sin made by Christ, for them there is no other. The author says in verse 26 that for these people there remains no more a sacrifice for sins.

Now what does all this mean for a doctrine of the Spirit? I take it that the Spirit of grace here is the Holy Spirit whose function it is, as seen in the Gospels, Acts, and Paul, to enlighten men as to the significance of Christ and his saving work. Through the word of the gospel, he gives to men a full knowledge (ἐπίγνωσις) of the truth. But if they reject this, there is no other remedy. This author all the way through has emphasized the danger of unbelief. Even in Old Testament times, men lost the blessing through an evil heart of unbelief (3:7-19). When one continues in a life of wilful unbelief after receiving such a full knowledge of the truth, there is nothing left for him except a looking forward to the fiery judgment of God.

Compare this with the warning that Jesus gave men concerning the danger of blasphemy against the Holy Spirit and eternal sin. Notice the same relation of the work of the Spirit to Christ and his gracious work. The Spirit is the Spirit of grace, not apart from Christ, but because he works to bring men into right relation with Christ. The Spirit of grace works to bring men into vital relations with the Son in whom grace and truth have their being (John 1:17).[4]

We do not have in this book Paul's mysticism, but we have something more closely akin to it than we have sometimes recognized. Turn back to chapter six and notice how the experience of entering the Christian life is described in verses 4-5. Christians are those who were once-for-all enlightened (by the Spirit evidently). The word for *once* enlightened is the same word that is used when this author says that Christ made a once-for-all offering for sin (9:12, 28). Here we have the same quality of finality (6:4 and 10:26) in the work of the Spirit that there is in the work of Christ. Christ made a once-for-all offering for sin. If one rejects that, there is no other. The Holy Spirit enlightens a man once-for-all with reference to Christ and his saving grace. If he rejects this, there is no other power that can

---

[4] It would be instructive to compare this also with what John calls the sin unto death (1 John 5:16-17).

give him light.[5] The finality, however, in the work of Christ and the finality in the work of the Spirit are not two and disconnected. They are one and the same—the finality of God in grace dealing with man for his salvation. If God's grace is rejected, there remains nothing for the sinner except the finality of justice and judgment.

One of the most notable features of the book of Hebrews in regard to the Holy Spirt is the manner in which the author refers to the Holy Spirit in relation to Old Testament Scripture quotations.

Sometimes he introduces a Scripture quotation or a summary of Scripture meaning in a rather casual manner, as when he says (2:6): "One hath somewhat testified" and quotes from Psalm 8. In chapter 4, he refers to a Scripture quotation or the meaning of Scripture as "he hath said." (See vv. 3, 4, 7 and 8:8.) Twice he quotes Scripture and refers it directly to the Holy Spirit as author. In 3:7, he says: "The Holy Spirit saith" and quotes Psalm 95. In 10:15, he says: "The Holy Spirit also beareth testimony" and quotes Jeremiah 31:33f. In 9:8, in setting out the plan and contents of the tabernacle of the Old Testament, he says: "the Holy Spirit this signifying."

Not only does this writer quote particular passages and refer them to the Holy Spirit as author,

---

[5]This is the reason the author says in 6:6 that those who fall away after being once-for-all enlightened cannot be renewed to repentance. They cannot be saved because they cannot be brought to repentance. It seems to me that there is a difference between the author's thought in 6:4ff. and in 10:26ff. In 10:26ff, he is speaking of one who is enlightened, but not renewed. In 6:4ff., he speaks *hypothetically*. He seems to be writing to those Jewish Christians who were being tempted to renounce Christ and go back to Judaism. He says in substance: "Suppose you should, what would you get? You would get nothing better. In fact, you would get *nothing*. You got all that Christ can do. If you throw that away, there is nothing left for you." His words following show that he expects better things of them. His is an *ad hominem* argument. See the paraphrase in Dana's *Jewish Christianity*.

but he also treats the whole Old Testament order of things, including the Old Testament itself, as of divine origin and as having divine significance. This he does in spite of the fact that he regards the Tabernacle (Temple) and the religious system connected with it as of transitory value. The value of this system lies in its preparatory nature. It has value only in its symbolical nature and in its preparation for Christ and his work.

Nevertheless, he does consider Old Testament Scripture as of God and as being produced by the Holy Spirit. It is divinely created. Such a passage as 9:8 (and the author's whole discussion of the Old Testament order) shows that he was not thinking, as some of our modern orthodox writers, of inspiration *in vacuo*, as an isolated transaction apart from the whole movement of which the writing of Scripture was a part. The writing of Scripture (and Scripture itself) has meaning only as seen and interpreted in relation to its background and the whole historical and social movement of which it was a part. That gives a legitimate and necessary place for historical and literary criticism in understanding and interpreting Scripture. This means that Scripture must be interpreted in relation to its context, in a broad but very definite sense. This author's treatment of Scripture justifies the recognition of historical development in interpreting and applying Scripture. What it does not justify is the emptying of all divine significance out of Scripture meaning.

What we are saying of this author in regard to the divine meaning of Scripture applies to Paul and New Testament writers as a whole. Jesus said (Mark 12:36) that David spoke in the Holy Spirit. He then quotes Psalm 110:1. Paul frequently quotes or refers to Scripture to prove a point. There are two explicit statements among the later writings of the New Testament bearing on the inspiration and authority of the Scriptures. One is in 2 Peter 1:20-21. Here the author says that no prophecy is of private interpretation. This probably means that one is not justified in putting his own individual construction on prophecy. This would certainly reduce many sermons and books to a surprisingly brief length. The reason that no man has a right to put his own individual construction on prophecy (or other Scripture) is that prophecy did not come by the impulse of man, but men spoke from God, being moved by the Holy Spirit. The Spirit puts more than an individual meaning in Scripture, a common or universal (i.e., a divine) meaning. It is more than human and individual; it is divine and universal.

In 2 Timothy 3:16, Paul says that all Scripture is given by inspiration of God. He then points out that as a result Scripture is profitable. It is profitable for teaching, for reproof, for correction, and for instruction (or discipline) in righteousness. I think Paul means that Scripture is profitable because it is inspired of God. He has just said that the Scriptures are able to make one wise unto salvation. Now he is saying that they are profitable for practical guidance in the ways of truth and righteousness.

Thus these writers, in line with the whole New Testament, tell us that the Scriptures are from God; that they are inspired by the Spirit; that they are God's creation. Second Peter includes Paul's writings under the head of Scripture (3:15). Everywhere else when Scripture is referred to, it means the Old Testament.

The fact set out by these writers explains that spiritual quality of the Bible that we do not find in any other literature in the world. To affirm the inspiration of the Bible does not explain, by any means, all the problems and perplexities which one meets in studying it. But it does help to explain its distinctive spiritual quality. It helps us to understand how the Bible is really in a class by itself, not in the forms of its literature, not in the realms of science, history and knowledge in general. But it does set this body of literature in a class of its own in relation to a knowledge of salvation through our Lord Jesus Christ and in the matter of Christian living.

III

The Apocalypse has some characteristics in common with the Gospel and First Epistle of John, but it is also quite different. The nature of the book, which no doubt was largely determined by the circumstances under which it was written, would help to explain the differences. One of these differences is that we find none of that intimate mysticism, commonly described as union with Christ, which is one of the central features of the Gospel and First Epistle.

We do find, however, some material on the place of the Spirit in the Christian life, both in relation to the individual and community life.

One strange conception in this book is that called the seven Spirits of God (1:4; 3:1; 4:5; 5:6). By some that is taken as another designation for the Holy Spirit. This is suggested by the trinitarian implication of 1:4. But there are some things about the use of the term that cause me to hesitate to accept the simple equation of the term with the Spirit of God or Holy Spirit. One is the fact that in general in Christian language in a trinitarian reference the Spirit was put last. So it is in Matthew 28:19 and 2 Corinthians 13:14.   This, however, would not be decisive, as the mode of the statement about the three Persons of the Trinity might very easily vary according to the requirements of the thought expressed, as we see from Ephesians 2:18.   But in a rather formal mention of the Persons of the Trinity, if this term denotes the Holy Spirit, such as we have here in 1:4, it would be more natural for the Spirit to be mentioned last.

But the term in all four of its uses is associated with the Eternal One, his throne, or with Christ, in such a way as to suggest that it is meant to designate a quality of divinity rather than a person in the Godhead.   It suggests rather the omnipotence or searching omniscience of God or Christ, whose divinity is made to stand out in this book.

Another noticeable expression is the one in which the author speaks of himself as being "in the Spirit" (1:10; 17:3; 21:10).   This might be regarded as almost a technical term to suggest the experience of a prophet in receiving a vision or revelation from God.   Paul seems to have had such visions. (See 2 Corinthians 12:1ff.)   And so did Peter.[6] (See Acts, chap. 10.)   This sounds very much like the experiences of the prophets of the Old Testament.   The writer of this book definitely means to put himself in the prophetic class.   He receives visions and revelations from God to encourage his persecuted and hard-pressed Christian brethren.   This expression "in the Spirit" might suggest a kind of trance-like

---

[6]Note also the experience of Jesus in being placed (in vision?) on a pinnacle of the Temple and a very high mountain (Matt. 4:1ff.; Luke 4:1ff.).

state in which the seer's whole being is possessed
and controlled by the divine Spirit. The first use of
the term in 1:10 is the most striking. The usual
translation here says: "I was in the Spirit." But the
more accurate way of putting it would be: "I *became*
in the Spirit." It would be the author's way of saying that on the Lord's Day, in his lonely vigil on the
isle of Patmos, perhaps as he meditated on the resurrection of Jesus on the first day of the week, which
commemorated his rising from the dead,[7] he came
under the sway of the Spirit and received the vision
of the living Lord which he records in the remainder
of chapter one. The other two uses of the term (17:
3 and 20:10) express the experience of the prophet
John as he is brought into enraptured fellowship
with the living Christ as he marches on to complete
victory in establishing his kingdom on a redeemed
earth.

In the letters to the seven churches, toward the
end of each message, there occurs the expression:
"He that hath an ear, let him hear what the Spirit
says to the churches" (2:7, 11, 17, 29; 3:6, 13, 22).

In these letters to the churches of Asia, it is the
living Christ who is speaking to the churches—the
Christ who manifested himself to John in the vision
recorded in chapter one. Different phases of his
character and activity are brought out in these letters. He seeks to manifest that aspect of his character and work that the particular church needs. The
hope of these struggling and distraught churches is
that the living Christ walks in their midst. No
church is hopeless so long as the living Christ is in
its midst. He is in the midst of these churches as
the One who searches, purifies, defends, and corrects

---

[7]See *Expositor's Greek Testament.*

them. But he works through the Spirit. It is through the Spirit that he seeks to communicate to them a knowledge of his will. The hope of these struggling, persecuted churches is in the living Christ. But the hope of the living Christ for his churches lies in the presence and power of the Spirit in the churches. The Spirit is speaking to them. He is trying to make known to them their needs, their weaknesses, their failures. He seeks to strengthen, guide, and build up the churches.

But the Spirit is limited by the lack of capacity on the part of the members of the churches to hear. A few can hear, but many cannot. He is searching for those who can. He is looking with searching eye for those who have capacity to hear the message of the Lord. That is the limitation against which the Lord and Master of the churches still struggles. He still hunts in the midst of the churches for those who have hearing ability. "He that hath an ear." We hear that same expression from Jesus while he was on earth in the flesh (Mark 4:9, et al). Now that he has returned as the living Lord in the Spirit, he is still calling, calling with pathetic voice, for those who can hear. There are so few of them, even in the churches. The great need of the churches is for those who can discern the will of the Lord of the churches as he speaks in the Spirit. Many of the churches are afflicted with heresy, with lethargy, threatened with worldliness, many with outright extinction as spiritual bodies because there are so few people in the churches who have spiritual sensitivity enough to hear and do what the Spirit says to the churches concerning the will of the living Lord in their midst. With many, his presence is not even discerned, his voice is not heeded. The hope of our churches today is in the presence in them of that small minority who can hear and heed the voice of the living Christ as he speaks to the churches through the Spirit.

Right at the end of this book (22:16-17), we hear Jesus, the offspring of David, calling to the churches; and we hear the Spirit joining with the churches, calling to the world, to any who thirsts, to come and take the water of life freely. Christ's hope of reaching the world is through the churches; and the hope of any evangelistic or missionary efficiency in the churches lies in the fact that the Spirit joins his voice with that of the churches in calling men to the living Christ who can satisfy the thirst of man for the water that gives life.

CHAPTER X

THE RELATION OF THE SPIRIT TO THE POWERS OF MAN

There are some special questions concerning the Holy Spirit and his work in the lives of men that need further consideration. These have been touched upon in our discussion so far, but they need some clarification. At the risk of some repetition, I would like to give consideration to two of these questions.

One is the question of the relation of the divine Spirit to the powers of man. We will consider that question in this chapter. In the last chapter we will discuss the question of the personality of the Spirit.

I

There are, as previously indicated, two extremes on this question. One is the extreme of holding to the sufficiency of man without the presence or power of God. This general position takes different forms. Some people who stress the authority of the Bible look on the Bible as a kind of road map that one needs to read only in a common sense way and follow directions. They reject anything like a mystical element in religion and regard Christianity as a kind of legal establishment. One is to read the Bible, find what has been prescribed as the conditions of salvation and obey, taking these conditions in proper order, and then rest on the promise of God to forgive and save. In like manner, one is to read the Bible to find what is required for Christian living and in a similar manner obey. This way of regarding the Christian life is legalistic, authoritarian, and "common sense." This type of thinking usually puts stress on the legal authority of the church. Valid Christianity depends, we are led to believe, on such authority. Whether the type of ecclesiology practiced is elaborate or simple, the advocates stress the validity of their particular church and regard all others as "sectarian." Salvation is closely connected with membership in this church, if not absolutely dependent on it. This type of thought has very little use for the indwelling and enlightening Spirit of God. It regards all talk about the power of the Spirit as fanatical. All a man needs to live a Christian life is common sense to interpret his road map and make the right turns at the right place.

Jesus had to deal with a legalistic religion, a religion of rules and regulations. Such a religion has small place, if any, for inner inspiration and power. Religion is a matter of being told what to do and how to do it. If one is told in a book or by a priest what to do, then if he does not do it, it is his fault. The devotees of such a religion always look with suspicion on a prophet who comes with a fresh message from God or who offers men new joy and power from fountains of inner inspiration.

There is another general attitude that places much emphasis on culture, education, and human self-development. This type of thought, if it recognizes God at all, does not acknowledge any direct and conscious fellowship of man with God. Man is expected to work out his own destiny within the general framework of the system in which he finds himself. In general, those who hold this attitude have received a considerable shock in the past generation. Two world wars and a worldwide economic debacle have shaken the confidence of many men in the ability of the human race to guide its own destiny. But there are still those who look to science and human culture to take care of man's needs. With these the emphasis is often on the laws of nature, the fixity of natural law, and with some the moral capacities of man. Some who hold this attitude believe in a faraway God, some emphasize the ethical and social teachings of Jesus, and some believe in a general immanence of the divine in human life. But there is a general coolness toward any belief in a special indwelling of the Spirit of God in the believer, furnishing him with light and power in the affairs of a workaday world. While one hesitates to make general accusations, the tendency of this attitude is toward a secularization of the whole of life, including religion itself. This is a subtle tendency and is not always immediately evident when it appears. It is the tendency on the part of man to make himself independent of any power other than, or higher than, himself. It has been operative in American religious life for sometime and has led to emptiness and sterility in much of our religious life. It is this kind of spirit that Paul has in mind when he talks about the wisdom of man as being foolishness with God and when he speaks of science falsely so called. It is the type of mind that does not wish to admit any dependence on God. This is different from the type described above as legalistic. That type looks to the Bible for a rule to do everything. This type rather feels no need for any kind of objective guidance.

II

There is an opposite tendency in religion which puts all the emphasis on God's power and makes man a passive instrument in the hands of the Divine. It was represented in our country in the past by what was popularly called "Hardshellism." It was confined mostly to the Baptist denomination and largely to the South. These people called themselves "Primitive Baptists." They put all the emphasis on the divine sovereignty and denied any efficacy to human effort. They did practically no missionary or evangelistic work, since they held that if God wanted anybody saved he would save him without the use of human means. They did not deny in theory the work of the Holy Spirit, but they did hold the helplessness of man in relation to the gospel and the Spirit. In theory, the Spirit did everything and man did nothing. What we have in this instance is rather paradoxical. It is a cancellation of divine power by a one-sided emphasis on divine power. Those holding this view nullified divine power by refusing it a means of communication. The power of God and human agency are related as a copper wire and electricity. Electricity does the work; human agency furnishes the connection. Some people see only the wire. They insist on the wire, human organization, and agency. Some others insist that it is the electricity that does the work. They, therefore, see no need of the wire. They have no use for organization and human agency. It was the inability of man that they stressed, and that is the point that we are now considering. Some views said man did everything. This view said that man did nothing. It practically denied that man could ever respond to God's grace offered in Christ. As a

result of their failure to do evangelistic and missionary work, they have almost passed out of existence.
Any form of religion that does not propagate itself
will necessarily die.

Another manifestation of the same general attitude is found among people who refuse to use
doctors or medicine in cases of illness, but believe
rather in divine healing. As in the case of the
"Hardshells," it is a question of the use of means.
In one case, it was a question as to whether God op-
erates mediately, through the gospel and human
agency for man's salvation or immediately, without
the use of means. In the other case, it is a question
as to whether God works immediately for healing
the body or whether he works through human agency
and material means. I take it that most any one of us
would be a little hesitant in either of these cases to
say what God could or could not do. But in view of
biblical revelation and two thousand years of history, one is perfectly safe in saying that in both
cases God ordinarily uses means to accomplish his
purposes. If one wanted to reduce this attitude to
logical consequences (as Mrs. Eddy did in theory,
but not in practice), why should he build houses, or
eat food? Why not disregard all material means for
preserving and enriching life? Why should not one
just disregard rain and, without seeking shelter, ask
the Lord to keep him dry? Some people insist that
going in a storm cellar out of a storm is a manifestation of a lack of faith in God. Would it not be as
reasonable to say that going into the house out of
the rain is due to lack of faith in God?

In the world of scholarship today, no doubt, the
best known example of this attitude is Karl Barth
and his kind. He maintains that in the fall the image

of God was obliterated so that there is nothing left in man to which the gospel can appeal. There is no connecting link between the nature of man and the gospel. Regeneration, so he maintains, is creation absolutely *de novo*. He will not allow that there is any basis in the moral nature of man on which God can work to produce the new man. The new man is an entirely new production.

In a personal discussion a number of years ago with an American follower of Barth, he maintained that if there were any basis in man's nature on which God could work, any connecting point for the gospel, then salvation would not be entirely by grace. There was no rational or moral spark of life to which God could appeal. I maintained that man was worth saving. He denied. It seems to me that we will have to distinguish between man's being worth saving and his being worthy of salvation. Unless man is worth saving, God engaged in a foolish enterprise when he sent Christ to save sinners. It amounts to about this. When God goes to make a saint, he does not begin *de novo*. He begins with the sinner that he has. Otherwise he would not be saving the sinner, he would be creating a new human being. That, in effect, is what Barth holds, as I understand it. He holds that when Paul talks about a man in Christ as being a new creation, he means literally a new creation, that Paul is not speaking figuratively. Barth and his followers deny there is in man by nature any capacity to respond to the gospel. Such capacity to respond, they hold, is a sovereign creation (shall we say, an arbitrary creation?) of God.

But the gospel is not addressed to a nonentity; it is addressed to a man who must respond. Paul represents himself as an ambassador speaking to men and saying, "We pray you in Christ's stead, be ye reconciled to God" (2 Corinthians 5:20). Paul entreats men. Why should Paul or any other servant of Christ entreat, persuade men, if there is nothing in them to which the gospel appeals, if there is no connecting point in man's rational or moral nature for the gospel? The gospel appeals to man's mind, man's conscience, man's will. It does not appeal to a thing or a mere animal, but to a man. The efficiency is of God, not of man. Legalistic religion and modern culture need to remember this. Paul may plant and Apollos water, but God must give the increase. Man cannot lift himself out of the quagmire of sin. God alone can do that. But it is man he lifts. The gospel appeals to sinners, but sinners are men, not things or animals. God has to make a man before the man can make himself a sinner. God can make a saint out of a sinner, but he cannot make a saint out of a vacuum. It seems to me that a large part of Barth's influence has been due to his intellectual keenness and vehemence and also to the absurdity of some of his positions. He appeared on the scene when there was a reaction overdue against our American practicality and humanistic religion. He shocked men into listening by the extreme lengths to which he went in his reaction against liberal theology in which he had been trained. Other men had been advocating a supernatural religion but had been setting it in such an intellectual atmosphere that they got no hearing. Barth came out of the liberal tradition and reacted against it in such a way as to get attention. Barth's system is educated "Hardshellism."

III

As to the relation, then, of the divine Spirit to the powers of man, our conclusion is that the Spirit of God lays hold of, interpenetrates, purifies, intensifies, and uses these powers. On the basis of such passages as 1 Corinthians chapter 1, in which Paul speaks of the wisdom of man as being foolishness in the sight of God, there has grown up a somewhat popular philosophy of religion that denied the legitimacy of the use of reason in the realm of religion. This type of thought has made many people afraid of ministerial education. This way of looking at the matter has been given dignity in the world of culture by Karl Barth and his followers. But it needs to be remembered that there is a difference between affirming the sufficiency of man's unaided reason in religion and denying altogether the legitimacy of the use of reason in the field of religion. Men sometimes appeal to reason to justify the rejection of the use of reason in the field of religion. In a corresponding manner, men sometimes deny the use of conscience and appeal to the Bible, the church, or some other wholly objective standard of right and wrong. To set the Bible over against conscience or reason and say that a man must choose between them is like saying that we must choose between light and eyes. Which does a man need in order to see, sunlight or eyes? Of course, he needs both. He might have all the light in the world, yet he could not see without eyes. On the other hand, one might have the best of eyes, yet he could not see without light. Sometimes we are told that one should not follow his conscience because conscience is fallible. One might make a mistake. What shall he follow? Let him follow the Bible or the church or some other standard, we are told. But whose interpretation of the Bible shall one follow? There are only two possible answers. I must follow either my own or submit myself to some priest or other functionary who proposes to interpret it for me. There are no other alternatives. If I act as a person, a morally responsible person, I must follow my own. I cannot act as a free and responsible person and do otherwise. Of course I may, I should, associate myself with others in my effort so to interpret the Bible or other standard offered. I will be ready to accept any help that comes. I will not be such an individualist as to think I can stand absolutely alone in history and society. I could not cut myself loose from the past or the social influences in the midst of which I live. I could not if I would. But in the last analysis, I must use my mind; I must make my own decisions. There is no rightful authority in religion—Bible, church, or any other—that relieves a morally free person from using his own mind or making his own moral decisions.

What I have been saying is what I understand Dr. E. Y. Mullins to have meant by what he called the competence of the soul under God in religion.[1] It means that in religion one must act as a responsible person. God deals with him as such. God deals with us as rational and moral beings. And he deals with us in order to develop our rational and moral powers. He wants to make us persons who are competent in the fields of truth and morals, in the field of religion. In acting personally in the field of religion, one is not to declare his independence of God. To do so is not to find freedom but slavery. To try to make oneself free from God in order to have personal com-

---

[1] See his discussion in *The Axioms of Religion.*

petence is like a bird seeking a vacuum in order that it may be free from the restricting atmosphere so that it may the better fly.

To say that one should follow his conscience is to say that he should always do what he believes to be right. Conscience is not a light that illumines man's inner life apart from light from without; it is rather the capacity within to recognize light and act accordingly. It is the power to judge one's actions according to the best light one has or can obtain. Jesus speaks about such a thing as blasphemy against the Holy Spirit. Does he not mean rejecting the light of God when one knows it as the light? Does he not mean deliberately calling white black? And does he not mean that one may burn out his moral nature until there is nothing left but a blackened, charred cinder, what Paul calls a seared conscience (1 Timothy 4:2)?

Paul recognizes in man an element that he calls spirit—something that may respond to the Spirit of God. This is the center of spiritual personality. This is quickened, remade, empowered by the indwelling Spirit of God. The Spirit of God is not given to man to displace man's mind, conscience, will; but to enable these to function properly, normally, in fellowship with God. A piece of cold steel becomes a different thing when heated to white heat. So are the powers of man when charged with the dynamic presence of the Spirit of God. There is an idea abroad in the world that for man to let God into his life means to pervert the human and keep it from being truly human. Nothing could be further from the truth. Man never existed apart from God. It is in him that we live, move, and have our being. The thing that perverts human life is the driving of God out, not letting him in.

The incarnation of God in Christ is the demonstration of the fact that man finds his true self-realization in union with God, not apart from him. The presence of God in the person of Jesus did not keep him from being truly human; rather it was the ground of his perfect and complete humanity. Jesus was a complete and perfect man, not in spite of the fact that he was divine, but because of that fact. No man is what he should be until God gets possession of him. When God, by his Spirit, enters, man is on the way to being what he should be as a man. God created man in the beginning. God can re-create him. Man can never be what he should be until God, by his indwelling Spirit, gets full possession.

IV

Of course, Paul does not expressly discuss the topic that we are here considering, that is, the relation of the divine Spirit to the powers of man. But there are some very definite implications in some things that Paul says. An examination of certain passages will show this. Some of these passages are: 1 Corinthians 2:10-16; 1 Corinthians chaps. 12-14; Romans 8:14-27; Romans 9:1; Ephesians 4:25-31. In fact, the whole discussion of Paul touching this question of the Spirit's work would bear on it. We have already discussed the passages previously cited, but there are certain features of these that need more explicit mention in this connection. Paul's use of the term spirit in man as found in 1 Corinthians 2:10-16 seems to imply that he is using it in the sense of man's consciousness or self-consciousness. Only a human consciousness (self-consciousness) can understand the things of man. The spirit of man alone can understand the things of man. In 1 Corinthians chapter 14, are some things that would, however, imply that man's spirit would include something like what modern psychology calls the subconscious. Paul contrasts praying in the spirit and praying with the understanding. Romans 8: 26-27 suggests the same thing. His language in the latter passage implies that there is a significance in our praying in the Spirit that cannot be grasped by the human mind or expressed in human language.[2] God reveals certain things to man by bringing them into man's mind, not by ignoring man's mind. The same thing is true in Ephesians 4:30 in regard to moral sensitiveness to right and wrong. The Spirit of God brings to man's mind a knowledge of truth, to his moral consciousness a sensitiveness as to right and wrong, to his spirit an assurance of sonship in God. All this he does by inhabiting man's inner life and illuminating his powers, not by ignoring them.

In his discussion of the convicting work of the Spirit as based on John 16:7-11, Dr. A. J. Gordon makes a contrast between conviction of the Spirit and the conviction of conscience.[3] There is some justification for this contrast, but it is liable to make a wrong impression about the convicting work of the Spirit. There is a practically universal sense in the hearts of men that something is wrong in their lives. Sometimes it is quite hazy and indefinite. To become evangelical conviction for sin, it must

---

[2]Cf. The position of William Sanday in regard to the subconscious as the place of the dwelling of the divine in Christ and that of William James as to the subconscious as the place of the divine working in man. Also cf. A. H. Strong: *Systematic Theology*, Vol. III, pp. 826ff.

[3]See *The Ministry of the Spirit*, pp. 187ff.

become something more definite and keen than a general sense of wrongness. That something definite comes under gospel influences by the power of the Spirit. But the Spirit does not bring this conviction to man apart from his own moral consciousness or conscience, but by quickening man's conscience. It is not gospel conviction for sin until the condemnation passed on the unbeliever by the gospel becomes the sinner's own self-condemnation. God's condemnation of the sinner must become the sinner's condemnation of self. The condemnation passed on man's selfishness, pride, and unbelief in the cross of Christ must have the sinner's "Amen" before he can pass out from under that condemnation. God's judgment of the sinner must become the sinner's judgment of himself. Any so-called salvation that did not change the sinner at the core of his moral being would be no salvation. It would leave the real man untouched.

While Dr. Gordon's discussion had particular reference to the passage in John 16, the position here held, that the work of the Spirit in man touches the very center of man's rational and moral nature, applies to the whole New Testament doctrine of the Spirit. This working of the Spirit is not something that moves on the plane of mechanical causation. It is not "scientific" in the strict sense of the word science. It is not contrary to science, but it moves on a higher plane than the operation of the forces of natural causation. It is more like the influence of person upon person. We speak of the indwelling and interpenetration of the Spirit in relation to man and his powers. But we are using spatial terms to suggest something that involves personal realities. Such language should be understood for what it is

—figurative and suggestive of something that is spiritual and personal. Only experience can verify the reality of it. But the experience of thousands has verified Paul's language.

Chapter XI

THE SPIRIT AS PERSONAL

One question concerning the divine Spirit that has been long debated is the question as to whether the Spirit is personal or impersonal. In general, it may be said that there are intimations in the Old Testament that the Spirit is personal, while in the New the personal nature of the Spirit comes out quite distinctly.

In the earlier part of the Gospels, however, especially the Synoptics, the view is impersonal, and no exact time can be designated when the view changes to the personal one. Perhaps about the earliest point when the Spirit is clearly set out as personal is in the farewell discourse of Jesus to the disciples in John 14-16. Here the view becomes clearly personal. In this farewell discourse, Jesus talks about the coming Spirit as if he were sending a warm, personal freind to be with them. In one or two places he uses a masculine pronoun, that one (Greek, ἐκεῖνος), to refer to the Spirit in spite of the fact that the antecedent word for Spirit (πνεῦμα) is neuter (14:26; 15:26; 16:7-8).

A word should be said about what is meant by personality. This is not meant as a full discussion, psychologically or philosophically viewed, as to the nature of personality. But it is easy to set out some of the fundamental and essential qualities of personality and to see from the data furnished by the New Testament and Christian experience that the Spirit possesses these qualities. We will mention

[177]

three of these.   They are intelligence, moral discrimination, and purposiveness.

If the Spirit is God, and God is personal, then the Spirit must be personal.   When we affirm that the Spirit is intelligent, then we are affirming that the Spirit is personal. A careful reading of Psalm 139 would show that God (or his Spirit) is regarded as intelligent—as omnipresent in his Spirit and also as omniscient.   This would suggest that, in a general sense, the Spirit must be regarded, even in the Old Testament, as having personal powers. The same thing is suggested by Isaiah 40:13-14.   Here directing the Spirit of Jehovah is about the same thing as being a councilor to teach the Lord or as instructing him or showing him the way of understanding. Passages like these, in the Old Testament no doubt influenced the thought of Paul in a statement like that recorded in 1 Corinthians 2:10ff.   In this passage, Paul identifies the power of understanding in both God and man with the Spirit of God on the one hand and with the spirit of man on the other.[1] We have also seen that in Romans 8:27 Paul speaks of the mind or thought of the Spirit, suggesting that there is a meaning in our praying beyond the meaning that we consciously put into it. That meaning (or intent) is that of the Spirit of God who guides us as we pray.   Here we have a suggestion as to how the overruling providence of God may be exercised in the life of the Christian—a providence that directs the Christian in ways and toward ends not seen by him.

The conclusion seems safe, then, that the Spirit of God possesses the quality of intelligence, since in both Old and New Testaments the Spirit is closely

---

[1]See chapter VII on Paul's teachings.

related to intelligence in God, if the two are not identified.

As to the second quality of personality proposed, there can be little doubt, from a Christian point of view, that the Spirit is characterized by moral discrimination. This much at least is involved in the title Holy as applied to the Spirit a few times in the Old Testament and quite a number of times in the New. In the last analysis, holiness in the moral sense can apply only to personal being; only in a secondary sense is holiness a quality of impersonal being. The same conclusion as to the moral nature of the Spirit is involved in the fact that the Spirit of God is also the Spirit of Jesus or of Christ (Acts 16:6-7; Romans 8:9). This is implied in the awful warning that Jesus gave to the Pharisees about the danger of blaspheming the Spirit. Their danger was the danger of disregarding or defying the ultimate moral power of the universe, of doing this in such a way as to destroy all power of moral discrimination in themselves. The Holy Spirit is the Power that convicts men of sin as related to Jesus as the Holy One, the ultimate revelation of God. God is light; and since Christ is the incarnation of God, he thereby becomes the light of the world. This Light is the clear expression of God's holy love, love without any trace of moral evil. Christ has become the highest ideal for men, and his Spirit the dynamic of goodness for the race. The entrance of his Spirit into man constitutes him a new man morally and spiritually, and his indwelling Spirit constitutes the dynamic for moral and spiritual progress in Christians.[2] The power that produces moral intelligence and sensibility in

---

[2] See the discussion on the Holy Spirit and the Christian's ethical life in chapter 7.

man must itself be of the nature of moral intelligence. Paul exhorts his readers not to grieve the Holy Spirit of God (Ephesians 4:30). Only a moral person can be grieved by sin and evil.

The third characteristic that we proposed for personality is purposiveness. This implies will. But when we say purposiveness, this suggests not only will, but moral will—will acting in the moral realm and for moral ends.

Do we have evidence that there is purposiveness in the dealing of the Spirit of God with men? We do not propose here to try to survey the whole field of the Spirit's activity from this point of view, but to look at two or three things. Consider such a statement as that of Paul in 1 Corinthians 12:11. The apostle is discussing spiritual gifts, particularly as seen in the church at Corinth. They are various, he says, and serve different functions. But he says that all these various gifts are wrought by the same Spirit who divides to each one severally as he (the Spirit) wills. A man's gift is not according to his will or choice but according to the will or choice of the Spirit. The Spirit is sovereign in his distribution of gifts. The nature of his gifts to men is not determined by what the man would like to be or do but what the Spirit chooses for him. A man's gift is not determined, at least not altogether, by his natural ability and inclinations. These may have something to do with it. They may determine the range within which the Spirit may assign one's functions in the church. But, in the last analysis, the Spirit's gifts are supernatural bestowments, and they are bestowed according to the Spirit's will, not the choice of the recipient. That comes out clearly in Paul's discussion of this question.

The same thing holds in God's dealings with men today. One man would rather follow a certain line, do a certain type of work, but he feels impelled to another line or form of work. If left to his own choice, he would (let us say) choose to be a pastor rather than an evangelist, but the Spirit impels him to be an evangelist or missionary. There are many men and women today who are just as definitely impelled by what they take to be the Spirit's leading to a certain type of work or field of service as did Jeremiah, Isaiah, or Paul. They are quite definitely convinced that the divine will is for them to go in a certain direction. And this they do, not because they choose that direction but in spite of the fact that they do not choose such, often in spite of their pleadings and prayers that they be allowed to go in a different direction. To them, as to the apostles and prophets of old, the divine will for their lives is something *assigned,* something to which they must conform their lives or be disobedient to the will of God.

There seems to be good evidence, then, that the Spirit of God possesses the fundamental powers of personal being—intelligence, moral discrimination, and purposiveness. This must be true if God is a Person and the Spirit of God is God himself coming into our world to accomplish his purposes. And this is the conception of the Spirit found in both the Old and New Testaments. It has been maintained by orthodox theology that the Holy Spirit is God as much so as the Father or the Son. The Spirit is not an impersonal influence or abstract power that God sends into the world, but God himself energizing in the world and human life.

II

But when this much is said, we have not solved all the problems. It may be that we have only raised some. When we apply to God or to the Spirit of God the category of personality, we are applying to God a concept with the limitations that apply to human personality, and thus may lead to a conception of divine personality that is misleading to say the least. Orthodox theology has always applied the concept of personality to the distinctions in the Godhead with some hesitation and reserve. We need to remember this in speaking of three Persons in the Godhead. There are three Persons in the Godhead, only if we remember that these three fundamental distinctions in the Godhead can be called persons in a modified sense. This is one place where pantheistic philosophy has raised a plausible objection to Christian theism. Christian theism has been criticised for saying that God was both one and three. But Christian theism has never said that God was one and three in the same sense. To say this would be a rational contradiction. Nor has Christian theism at its best ever said that the distinctions in the Godhead were persons in the same sense that three human individuals were persons. To put it differently, the three distinctions in the Godhead may be spoken of as three Persons; they should not be conceived as three individuals.[3] It is to be feared that this has been true in the minds of both the friends and the opponents of trinitarian theology. One suspects that this is true when he hears talk about the councils of eternity, the office work of different persons of the Trinity, and sepa-

---

[3] On this point, see *Christianity and Personality*, by John Wright Buckham, pp. 85ff.

rate dispensations of the persons of the Trinity in
history. Men have talked about the councils of
eternity as if three individuals sat down together
around a table and worked out a plan, and we hear
about three dispensations and the office work of
the three Persons of the Trinity as if these three
individuals agreed that one of them should do his
work and stop; and then the second would do his
work and stop; and then the third would take up
his part and complete the undertaking. This comes
very near to a tritheistic conception of God. Over
against this we must never forget that the fundamental conception of God in the Bible is the unity of
God. The Lord our God is *one* Lord—not two,
nor three, but one. So taught Jesus and the New
Testament, as well as the Mosaic law and the Old
Testament.

There are two fundamental aspects of human personality—the individual and the social. The individual is that aspect that is exclusive and unsharable.
It is that aspect of the person that constitutes each
one a unit distinct from every other living unit.
It is that about each person that cannot be imparted
to another. It is the wall in consciousness that marks
the immovable boundary between each person and
his fellow. It is a wall around each man's conscious
self that marks it off to itself and constitutes its
peculiarity—a wall over which one cannot climb.
One may feel at times as if he would like to get over
that wall into the inclosure of his neighbor's consciousness and see things as his neighbor does and
feel life as he does. But he can never climb that wall.
Even the closest companions and friends must remain forever distinct and to a certain extent ex-

clusive. This aspect of personality constitutes individuality.

The other aspect of human personality is the social. Every human being is born and nurtured in a social matrix. Every human individual is also social in nature. The theologians have had a theory that angels were each a separate creation of God rather than being a race. Whatever may be true of angels, this is not true of human beings. We are members of a race, of nations, families, and of numberless other groups. There can be no personal life that is altogether and purely individual. Human personality is essentially social. Even Robinson Crusoe on a lonely island had to have his Friday in order to live a life that was to any extent truly human. Men have debated whether the gospel of Christ was intended to save the individual or change social conditions, sometimes not noticing that on either side they were debating an abstraction. The individual apart from society or society apart from the individual is an abstraction and has no concrete reality.

It seems to me that in the past we have interpreted the Trinity too much in individualistic terms. We have said that there were three Persons in the Trinity, but we meant three individuals. God is infinite and there can be in the nature of the case only one infinite. There cannot be three individuals in the Trinity.

The older theologians expressed this matter by saying that there was one essence in the Godhead, but that all the essence of the Godhead belonged to each of the three Persons of the Godhead. All the essence of the Godhead, we were told, belonged to the Father and all of it belonged to the Son and all to the Holy Spirit.

As I understand it, this was an effort to say that neither Person of the Godhead was God to the exclusion of the others, that neither excluded but rather included the others. This way of putting the matter may be too materialistic. It seeks to express the matter in terms of essence or substance rather than in terms of personal life.

One effort to express the matter in terms of personal life might be something like this. An infinite, solitary monad would not be a person. He (or it) would be only a non-personal or subpersonal thing, not a person.

III

It might help us to approach the question of the Trinity from the standpoint of the social aspect of personality. Each of the Persons of the Trinity lives in and for the others. Even a human person can live a worthy personal life only as he gives himself to and for others. Such giving is the thing that constitutes human life akin morally and spiritually to the divine. Our giving of self to and for others is grounded in the unlimited self-giving of the Persons of the Trinity to and for each other.

In interpreting personality as applied to the Trinity, emphasis must be put, then, on the unitive aspect of personality, not on the separative or exclusive aspect. As seen above, finite personality finds its development and completion in that form of self-giving that we call love. Love is self-giving —self-giving in accordance with the principles of righteousness. It is self-giving that is prompted by the good of the object to whom one gives self. There is in human relations something called love that is falsely so called. It is prompted by the desire to get, to possess the object or person loved. The motive of such love is self and to that extent it is not true love. Such love often degenerates into lust. In that case, the person loved is made a means to the end of pleasing oneself. True love in human relations is a mutual self-giving prompted by the desire to bless the object loved. In such love, the true blessedness of the lover is found in the welfare and happiness of the loved one. Such love has the element of sacrifice in it. The lover stands ready to sacrifice the happiness of self for the good of the loved one. If it is not thus unselfish, it fails to that extent and for that reason to be true love.

The purest demonstration of such love is found in God's giving of self to and for lost men in Christ. God so loved that he gave his Son, and in giving his Son he gave himself. So John and the other New Testament writers thought of it. Some men have so interpreted the cross as almost, if not quite, to make the impression that they thought that God gave his Son to avoid giving himself. No, just the opposite. God gave himself in giving the only begotten (only) Son. Who can think of the Father as giving his Son without giving himself? Who can think of the Son as dying on the cross in agony and shame and at the same time think of the Father who gave him as a cold impassive and impassible Being standing to one side in stoic indifference? Such a God is the Greek Zeus, not the biblical God and Father of our Lord Jesus Christ. In trinitarian terms, we might think of the God and Father who gave himself to man in Christ as giving himself to the Son in eternal and uncreated relationship. **God's** giving of himself to his only Son in unlimited fulness might be thought of as the archetypal prototype of his giving himself to mankind in Christ. In that case, God's self-giving to mankind may be thought of as grounded in his eternal self-giving to the Son. Creation and redemption might thus come to be seen as grounded in the trinitarian relations in the Godhead.

It is probably easier to see the trinitarian aspect of the Godhead as between the Father and the Son than it is as it applies to the Spirit. But in an effort to interpret the matter, we might begin with the work of the Spirit as seen in the New Testament and in Christian experience. Paul says in Ephesians 2:18 that we both (Jew and Gentile) through him (Christ) have access in one Spirit unto the Father. God comes to us in his Son; we come to God in the Spirit. It is only in and through the Spirit that we find access to God and fellowship with him. That is not a matter of speculation. That is a matter of experience. This is not the Spirit's work, however, apart from the Father and the Son, nor to the exclusion of the Father, and the Son, but in union with them. The Son does not redeem us apart from the Father, nor does the Spirit regenerate and sanctify apart from Christ. The work of the Son is the work of the Father, and the work of the Spirit is the work of the Son. The work of one is the work of all, and each works in and through the others. There is no office work of any Person of the Trinity that is not also the work of the other Persons of the Trinity. Creation, preservation, providence, redemption—all are the work of the undivided and indivisible Godhead.

IV

The Spirit may be spoken of as a Person. Yes, but not a separate personality. He is a Person only in relation to the other Persons of the Godhead. When the Spirit deals with us, it is a personal power, not an impersonal influence or power. Not only is it a personal power dealing with us, but it is the Power who is the source and ground of all personal existence in the universe; the Power who works to make us the right kind of persons, not apart from one another and from God, but in union with all other human persons and with God. It is in and through the work of this creative, sanctifying Power that we are brought into union with God and one another. In the great beyond it may be that we shall, through this creative and sanctifying Spirit of God, be brought into spiritual fellowship with all other created spirits who live in union with the God who is the source, support, and end of all things.[4]

---

[4] See the definition of God in *Systematic Theology*, Vol. I, p. 52, by A. H. Strong.

FOR FURTHER READING

In addition to the regular treatises on Systematic Theology, I would suggest that those wishing to read further on this subject might consult the following works.

I. ON THE OLD TESTAMENT

Davidson, A. B., *The Theology of the Old Testament*
Knudson, A. C., *The Religious Teachings of the Old Testament*
Snaith, Norman H., *The Distinctive Ideas of the Old Testament*

II. ON THE NEW TESTAMENT

Beyschlag, Willibald, *New Testament Theology*, 2 vols.
Sheldon, Henry C., *New Testament Theology*
Stevens, George B., *The Theology of the New Testament*
Stevens, George B., *The Pauline Theology*
Stevens, George B., *Johannine Theology*
Weiss, Bernhard, *Biblical Theology of the New Testament*, 2 vols.

III. SPECIAL WORKS ON THE HOLY SPIRIT

Carroll, B. H., *The Holy Spirit*
Chadwick, Samuel, *The Way to Pentecost*
Conner, W. T., *What Is a Saint?* (booklet)
Cummings, James E., *Through the Eternal Spirit*
Dana, H. E., *The Holy Spirit in Acts*
Davison, W. T., *The Indwelling Spirit*
Denham, W. E., *The Comforter*

Dillistone, F., *The Holy Spirit in the Life of Today*

Gordon, A. J., *The Ministry of the Spirit*

Greenfield, John, *Power from on High* (an account of the Moravian Movement)

Johnson, E. H., *The Holy Spirit Then and Now*

Hayes, D. A., *Speaking in Tongues*

Hoyle, Birch, *The Holy Spirit in St. Paul*

Jones, E. Stanley, *The Christ of Every Road*

Kuyper, Abraham, *The Work of the Holy Spirit*

Lawrence, J. B., *The Holy Spirit in Missions* (pamphlet)

Rees, T., *The Holy Spirit in Life and Experience*

Robinson, Wheeler, *The Christian Experience of the Holy Spirit*

Rouse, W. T., *The Holy Spirit*

Streeter, B. H. (ed.) and others, *The Spirit*

Swete, H. B., *The Holy Spirit in the New Testament*

IV. BOOKS ADVOCATING THE MODERN "HOLINESS" VIEWS

Brockett, Henry E., *Spiritual Freedom from Sin* (Nazarene)

Byrum, R. R., *Christian Theology* (Church of God)

Corlett, D. Shelby, *The Meaning of Holiness* (Nazarene)

Pearlman, Myer, *Knowing the Doctrines of the Bible* (Assemblies of God)

See also *The Path of Perfection,* by W. E. Sangster

INDICES

I. INDEX OF SUBJECT

II. Index of Authors

III. INDEX TO SCRIPTURE REFERENCES